Healing the Father-Wound

Bishop Steven W. Banks

Healing the Father-Wound

AND HE SHALL TURN THE HEART OF THE FATHERS
TO THE CHILDREN, AND THE HEART OF THE
CHILDREN TO THEIR FATHERS
MALACHI 4:6

BISHOP STEVEN W. BANKS

EXPANDING YOUR VISION
PUBLISHERS

VIRGINIA BEACH, VIRGINIA

Unless otherwise noted, all scripture quotations are taken from the King James Version of the Bible. Some scripture quotations marked "amp" are taken from the Amplified® Bible. Copyright© 1954, 1958, 1962, 1964, 1965, 1987 by the Lockman Foundation. Used by permission. (www.lockman.org).

Some quotations from the Scripture contain words emphasized by the author. These words are not emphasized in the original Bible version.

Life Application Bible
American Standard Bible
The Living Bible
New International Version of the Bible
NKJV Version of the Bible

Research on some Scriptures was found in the Unger's dictionary, Vines Concordance, and the Complete Book of Quotes.

09 08 07 06 05 04 10 9 8 7 6 5 4 3 2 1

Healing the Father-Wound
WWW.HEALINGTHEFATHERWOUND.ORG

ISBN 978-0-9817488-2-5

SWB Ministries

Expanding Your Vision Publishers

Fire Sky Media & Technologies, Pvt., Ltd, India
Consuming Fire Media & Technologies, LLC

I am honored and very proud to support my husband, Bishop Steven W. Banks, in the release of his monumental written work, *Healing the Father-Wound.* Steve is a man of great substance, wisdom, and integrity. As his wife of twenty-three years, I know my husband to be a man of great conviction and a strong believer. I know that he believes in a God whose mercy and compassion is available to all. I know he also believes in the blessing and the importance of marriage and family. He believes in his children and in their hopes and dreams. Ultimately, he believes that every day he is called to leave the world a little better than he found it.

Steve's path to healing and wholeness has not been an easy one. When I met my husband so many years ago, Steve was courageously dealing with the pain of his past. I also saw the beginning of his process towards restoring broken family relationships and trusting God for healing, forgiveness and renewal. *Healing the Father-Wound* is borne out of my husband's search for a place of restoration and wholeness and serves as a light to guide others along this same path. This book is also about identifying a pervasive condition that is all too often expressed through unmanaged anger, escapism and addictions, broken relationships with the opposite sex, and emotional disconnection. Furthermore, *Healing the Father-Wound*, for my husband, is a personal triumph and a testimony to the grace of God which looks beyond our human weaknesses and celebrates the divinity within us.

As a voice in favor of the restoration of the woman in this hour of Kingdom advancement, I am privileged to endorse *Healing the Father Wound*. I believe that when men are emotionally healed, the cycle of emotional wreckage and dysfunction upon the entire family is broken; vital relationships are restored, marriages flourish, and families are redeemed. This is a book written for men, but it is really about all of us.

Dr. Keira Taylor-Banks
Pastor, Author, and Television Host

If I had to describe my father in one word, that word would be consistent. He's consistent in his walk with God, in his loyalty to family, in his compassion, in his viewpoints, and in his role as provider. This quality, among many others, makes me proud to call him "Dad". I've always felt a certain amount of pressure with being the only daughter of a well-known Bishop. But the older I become, the more I realize that his role of "Father" was just as important, if not more important than his role of "Bishop". Never once, did I feel as though my father judged me because of my shortcomings. He has always uplifted and encouraged me and will continue to do so, even when I face new challenges. And I know this as truth because he's been consistent thus far, and I love him for that.

KEIRA IMAN BANKS

My dad is my hero, because he is very intelligent. He takes care of me when I need help. He is a brave man, because he is fearless. He is willing to give to other people. He makes me feel fantastic when he supports me in everything I'm involved in.

My dad loves me no matter what and I love him back always.

JORDAN IMANUEL BANKS

Congratulations to Bishop Steven W. Banks on your new book, *Healing the Father-Wound.* We live in a world that hurts and hates because of the wounds of fathers. In Luke 9:11 we are given a very powerful image of Jesus' desire to heal. "And the people, when they knew it, followed Him: and He received them, and spake unto them of the kingdom of God, and healed them that had need of healing". I trust every one of us will receive help and healing through the revelation of this book, *Healing the Father-Wound.*

NATE HOLCOMB
Christian House of Prayer Ministries and
Presiding Bishop, Covenant Connections International, Inc.

Steven Banks has written an insightful and accurate description of a key psychological issue that affects most members of our society today. The Father-Wound, as he describes it, is something I see and address frequently with patients. Steven's approach is compelling and full of practical wisdom to help people heal and be whole.

JEFFREY GARDERE, PH.D
Psychologist, Author and Television Commentator

Having done extensive counseling and hosted many marriage conferences, I have witnessed first-hand the devastation of the fatherless generation. I believe Bishop Banks is being used of God to put his finger on one of the primary dysfunctions facing the Christian home.

Ron Carpenter Jr. Founder/Senior Pastor
Redemption World Outreach Center, Greenville, SC

Healing the Father-Wound can lead to a better understanding of our internal emotional conflicts, and provide a path for a more fulfilling relationship with our significant other. Through Bishop Banks' work we gain a greater understanding and appreciation of the importance of fathers' affirmation in the healthy development of their children.

Jeremiah Williams, Ph.D, LCSW
Marriage and Family Therapist

I am so excited to write this endorsement because I believe that Bishop Banks has tapped into an area of the spirit that will truly release years of pain and bring deliverance to the blood line of many. God has blessed Bishop to be able to give name to the generational dysfunction of many. I dare say that almost everyone has been affected by a Father-Wound directly or indirectly. This is not just a book but an eternal offering to God. We celebrate that this offering has a high call to heal wounds, bring peace and manifest clarity for all who will embrace the truth in which it releases.

Dr .K. W. Brown, Senior Pastor
The Mount, Chesapeake, VA

In his book, *Healing the Father-Wound*, Bishop Steven Banks, not only identifies the wounds, but through spiritual precision and acute attention, provides healing and hope for a world with Father-Wounds. This work is not just theory, but a testament to the authenticity of the principles of Fatherhood that Bishop Banks has provided for my own life. Get ready to be fathered from woundedness into a new place of wholeness.

Dr. David B. Mills
Through the Word Bible Fellowship, Chester, PA
National Director, Living Waters International Alliance

Bishop Steven Banks provides a reflective look at the effects of not having the affirmation of your father. This is a heartfelt book for any and everyone – fathers, sons, daughters, brothers, sisters and even mothers. This insight is much needed for the Body of Christ.

Bishop Lyle Dukes, Senior Pastor
Harvest Life Changers Church, Woodbridge, VA

Early in my career, I was an attorney working in the family courts in New York and had a chance to see first-hand the physical effects of absentee fatherhood manifested in the form of extreme juvenile delinquency (rape, robbery assault, and teen pregnancy). Bishop Steven Banks is a true prophet of God who, in his new book, has tapped into an area of great concern for the Body of Christ and filled it with the word of God and revelation to heal the sin-sick soul.

Attorney D. Boyd Jones
Global Justice Ministries

Bishop Steven Banks has written a superb book that should be required reading for anyone interested in restoring the hearts of the fathers to their children… In very descriptive and stylistic language, Bishop Banks has captured a culture that has been tucked away and unexposed for too long. This well-written book exposes our ontological wounds and our existential bruises as it addresses the brokenness millions have endured at the hand of absentee fathers. This important work is a game-changer for those searching for answers in the often complex world of father-son/father-daughter relationships.

The Rev. Dr. Earl C. Johnson, Senior Pastor
Martin Street Baptist Church, Raleigh, North Carolina

I believe that through the revelation shared within the book, God has allowed Bishop Banks to expose the root of many challenges that people are facing today. Regardless as to whether you would characterize your relationship with your father as positive or challenging, the relationship has an effect on where you are today. This book, *Healing the Father-Wound*, is critical and paramount to your success.

BISHOP DANIEL ROBERTSON, JR.
Mount Gilead International Full Gospel Ministries, Richmond, VA

What a timely masterpiece addressing the epidemic and impact of the absence of fathers in the lives of their children. Bishop Steven Banks definitely heard from God and recorded the words in this book entitled *Healing the Father-Wound*. As a result of reading this book, the hearts of fathers will be drawn to their sons and daughters and the hearts of the children will be reconnected to their fathers. This book is more about restoration and healing than exposing the symptoms or flaws of men. Read it and be blessed!

CHARLIE AMMONS, ASST. PASTOR
Living Waters Christian Fellowship, Newport News, VA

Healing the Father-Wound, is a book with Apostolic foundations - tearing open the prison doors, rescuing the captives, revealing our emotional diseases, so as to begin the healing process. In his book, Bishop Banks masterfully reveals the hurts from absentee, emotionally withdrawn or abusive fathers. Sadly, we haven't known where to go... Bishop Banks supplies wise direction.

ELDER CORNELIA BROWNING-MOORE
M.Div., LCSW, MSW

In a fatherless world where men abdicate their roles and shun their responsibilities, gaping wounds, as a result, have occurred, creating hurt in the hearts of men and women, causing them to hurt others. This book, *Healing the Father-Wound* articulates the societal ills such as abuse, abandonment, and addictions, and brings forth healing for the inner soul. I am convinced this book will navigate you into a life of wholeness. Read with GREAT EXPECTATION!

Dr. Dexter Howard
Founder/Pastor of Life Harvester Church International Outreach

Healing the Father-Wound is a practical resource to begin the journey towards emotional and spiritual wellbeing. It is a tragedy that many in our communities and churches believe that ignoring a wound by pretending it is not there will allow it to heal on its own. Although that strategy may work for minor emotional and spiritual wounds, it is not effective to ignore a gaping wound that impacts a person's sense of self and how they relate to others… Through this book, the readers will be able to identify the problem, symptoms, and treatment to begin the active process towards emotional and spiritual healing.

Patrice Turner, Psy.D.
Clinical Psychology Resident

One of the greatest pandemics and the gravest problems of this generation is the absence of fathers in so many families across the globe. However, there is an uncompromisingly desperate need across every culture, tribe and tongue for a healthy father-figure in the lives of each and every individual son and daughter. Bishop Banks has put forth a significant and comprehensive study of this most imperative subject, providing practical solutions and taking a biblical and balanced approach that shows us how to identify, reckon with, and heal some of the deepest wounds of our lives.

Bishop Daniel Dayanandhan
Synod of the Independent Christian Churches of Asia
Asia International Ministers (AIM) Fellowship

Bishop Banks' book is the antidote to many of the ills in society that have caused men and women to fall short of their destinies in life. *Healing the Father-Wound* exposes the genesis of the hurts and pains that many of us have tried to camouflage through exterior outlets such as drugs and sexual addiction, among other vices; without seeking a permanent cure. Bishop Banks, through the guidance of the Holy Spirit and his personal experiences has provided every lost man or woman an opportunity to gain restoration and redemption from the pain they suffered from their fathers. I applaud Bishop Banks for courageously addressing an issue that many men and women find too sensitive to confront due to the emotional and psychological wounds that have been perpetual since childhood. To that end, *Healing the Father-Wound* pardons the wounds and provides emancipation to a generation of wounded adults who can truly ascertain their identities and attain the goals that have been preordained by our Heavenly Father.

Attorney Melvin Wright Jr.

In a time where some father's are absent but desperately needed, Bishop Banks has done an awesome job in writing this book and revealing to us the importance of having a fatherly connection. We all know someone with a father wound or have experienced it ourselves. This is a powerful read and must be shared with every man that's a father or father to be, for it will touch his life and many generations to come.

Pastor John C. Green
Sr. Pastor, Victory by Faith Church

Fathers certainly have the ability to either effect positive or negative influence on their children. Bishop Banks has laid out a very detailed and exhaustive statement on how fathers can use their God-given position to truly show our Heavenly Fathers' heart and how we can as fathers follow His example.

Pastor Randy Gilbert
Faith Landmarks Ministries, Richmond, VA

Healing the Father Wound is a timely, God inspired book which speaks to the silent pain that many people suffer flowing from a rupture in the father child relationship. As we turn to God for guidance and forgiveness of our own short comings, we can in love forgive imperfect fathers who like all of us fall short.

Jonathan K. Stubbs, J.D., LL.M., M.T.S.
Professor of Law, University of Richmond School of Law

WWW.HEALINGTHEFATHERWOUND.ORG

This Book is Dedicated

To

The men I've always loved and admired

Robert S. Blueford

Harold A. Banks

Rev. Dr. James R. Taylor

William P. Blueford

Robert S. Blueford Jr.

# *Acknowledgments*

I would like to thank my team for assisting me with this book, "Healing the Father-Wound." I am profoundly grateful for your great support and professional contributions to this written work.

Reganda Smith
Mary Holloway
Blisson Thangamani
Stephen Blackmon
Dr. Patrice Turner
John Conley
Deborah Hunter
The Team at FireSky Media and Technologies

I would also like to acknowledge my wife, Dr. Keira Taylor-Banks for her unwavering love and encouragement towards this assignment. Also all my heart and love to my amazing children, Keira Iman and Jordan Imanuel.

Contents

1. Father-Wound Syndrome 33

2. The Power of Affirmation 45

3. Fathers and Daughters 69

4. Fatherless Daughters 81

5. The Truth About Relationships 99

6. The Father's Blessing 113

7. Emotional Connection 141

8. You Are Not Alone 155

9. Satisfying the Father-Hunger 165

Foreword

A couple of years ago I had a very interesting conversation with a young African student. He was in this country to attend college and while matriculating at St John in New York he played on their basketball team. This student/ athlete shared with me his opinion that the absent black father has had a devastating impact on young black males. He concluded that so many young black men have anger issues and issues with authority figures as a result of wounds that were created by the absent father.

Bishop Steven W. Banks has taken on this issue in a clear, concise, informative, sensitive, and powerful way. He surfaces the trauma and challenges that these father wounds have made, but more importantly he shares with the reader ways that can cause the healing to begin. As a spiritual leader Bishop Banks shares direction and guidance for both the man/child who has been wounded and the father who had done the wounding can be reconciled to each other and reconciled to God. In every approach that is suggested accompanying scripture is given that makes it clear that this is strong Christian teaching that has stood the test of time.

This work will prove to be a blessing to many. It will be a helpful read for young and old alike. It really focuses on how to build the father and son relationship, but it will be a great asset for all relationships within the context of the family. I recommend this work to soon to be and new fathers. I recommend it to seasoned father who want to do a better job of fathering. I recommend to all Men's Ministries, and I recommend to all mothers who want to have a better understanding of the needs of the boys in their lives.

Bishop John R. Bryant
Senior Bishop AME Church

Introduction

"We need fathers to realize that responsibility does not end at conception. We need them to realize that what makes you a man is not the ability to have a child – it's the courage to raise one."

Barack Obama
President of the United States of America

This book will bring tremendous insight and healing to the readers. As I released this to our local congregation, I realized that this was more than a sermon to be preached within the church. It is a message to all men; black, white, rich, poor, educated, uneducated, Christian, Muslim, Hindu or Jew. This is a message that crosses race, religion, age, and culture. To this text, I bring my uniqueness. I am an African–American, educated man who was reared by a single parent. I am a husband, a father of two children, and a Bishop. Yet, what you are about to read is not restrictive to only those who share my uniqueness. This message transcends my uniqueness and speaks to all men. There will be some jargon that's akin to my profession and calling; however, I will clarify and expound upon the terminology, so that you may understand the meaning. Ultimately, this is not a Sunday-go-to-meeting message, but it is a message for this prodigal generation in search of meaningful relationships.

Restoration is defined *as the act of bringing back something to its former condition or original intended state*. Within the House of God, we describe this as *revival*. **Revival** is understood *as the act of restoring, refreshing, recalling, or returning to a former consciousness or life*. The Old Testament prophet Elijah embodies this spirit. The major part or primary function of the spirit of Elijah in this hour and these last days will be to bring about the restoration of relationships between the father and his children. Malachi 4:5 states, "The spirit of Elijah *shall* turn the heart of the fathers to the children and the heart of the children to the fathers." This **turning** means to *heal and to restore the relationship between fathers and their children*. Only the spirit of Elijah operating in the earth realm can accomplish this restoration of relationship.

This book will be a journey of discovery, healing, and restoration for you. Mainly, I will be addressing the father and son relationship. I have also included a chapter that specifically addresses the father and daughter relationship. Even though my primary focus is on the father and son relationship, I've been grateful that so many women have been helped through this message as well. Additionally, I will identify specific father-wounds and provide methods to assist you in your healing.

The Father-Wound is a topic that I am familiar with personally. When I was 13 years old, I met my father, Harold A. Banks Sr., for the very first time. It was an awesome experience! We had very little contact thereafter, until I turned 16 and reconnected with him. Every summer, I would go to visit him in Philadelphia where he lives with his wife, Naomi of over 30 years. I had no idea that God was restoring our father-and-son relationship and making it into what it is today.

I recently visited my father in Pennsylvania, and I interviewed him for the purpose of this book. I also had an opportunity to interview my father-in-law, Rev. Dr. James R. Taylor. I believe that their stories will give added depth to what will unfold.

God has entrusted me with the responsibility to *raise men*. I am called to develop fathers into their fatherhood. Writing about the father and son relationship is part of my assignment. As you read *Healing the Father-Wound*, I believe that God is going to release understanding and healing into your life. You will comprehend your assignment and grasp the importance of being involved in the lives of your children. In addition, you will recognize your responsibility to make an impartation into their lives – spiritually, physically, emotionally, and financially.

Come with me on a journey into restoration and wholeness!

Bishop Steven W. Banks

Chapter One

THE FATHER-WOUND SYNDROME

One night a father overheard his son pray, "Dear God, Make me the kind of man my Daddy is." Later that night, the father prayed, "Dear God, Make me the kind of man my son wants me to be."

~Author Unknown

Behold, I will send you Elijah the prophet before the coming of the great and dreadful day of the LORD: And he shall turn the heart of the fathers to the children, and the heart of the children to their fathers, lest I come and smite the earth with a curse.

Malachi 4:5-6

According to the scripture, the prophet Malachi foresees a time when the heart of the fathers will be turned to their children and the heart of the children to their fathers. We are in this moment of time. Like no other time in history, this generation is marked by broken relationships and broken hearts. The prophetic words in The Book of Malachi speak of two realities: first, it speaks of estranged or *cursed* relationships, and secondly of relationships restored. Today, father and son relationships are severely damaged and in many cases non-existent. The fallout from these broken and challenged relationships is a host of disconnected individuals suffering privately from a *father-wounds.*

Men of Honor

> *Honour thy father and thy mother, as the LORD thy God hath commanded thee; that thy days may be prolonged, and that it may go well with thee, in the land which the LORD thy God giveth thee.*
>
> *Deuteronomy 5:16*

Scripture gives great importance to honoring our fathers and mothers. For many, your father may be miles away, may be unknown, incarcerated, or deceased.

> *Whoso curseth his father or his mother, his lamp shall be put out in obscure darkness.*
>
> *Proverbs 20:20*

This word **curse** means to *make light of.* Used in this context, it means to *lightly esteem* your father and mother. It denotes that you do not hold them in high regard. Many people do not hold their fathers in high regard. For some, it is because of the pain they are experiencing internally. Many individuals have been wounded by their father's absence or his abusive behavior displayed towards them, their siblings, or their mothers. That is one reason why we normally see celebrities on TV win an award and acknowledge their mothers, but rarely their fathers. They will give honor to God first and then thank their mothers. Why is there a lack of honor for fathers? This will be addressed throughout the book.

There is a blessing attached to honoring your father and mother. It is a commandment from God, not an option. Those who are obedient to this commandment receive the blessing of an extended life.

One day last summer, I got the opportunity to do something nice for my father. I asked my dad, Harold A. Banks Sr., if we could pick him up and go into New York City for the day. To his surprise, my son and I pulled up in a white limousine. Dad didn't even recognize us and started to go back into the house. When he finally saw us, we all laughed. We went into the city and had a great time.

My father tells me that was one of his absolute best days. However, to be honest, I think I had the better time. It felt *great* to openly honor my father. Furthermore, my son Jordan was blessed to spend time with his father and grandfather and see the joyful interaction between my father and I. It is not in how much money you spend (though you should not run from spending money either), but it is about having a heart to respect your parents. There are innumerable blessings multiplied in your life when you choose to honor both your mother and father. Parents do not have to be perfect for us to honor them, and God honors our obedience to His Word.

God has promised, "If you honor your mother and father, I will prolong your days." However, the sad reality within our communities is the demonstration of a lack of honor for fathers. For example, on Mother's Day, flowers and merchandise sales skyrocket, along with card sales. People, who do not attend church regularly, show up on Mother's Day. They make it a point to send their mothers flowers, cards, chocolate, and jewelry. You name it and mothers get it for Mother's Day, and rightfully so. Some statistics regarding Mother's Day report:

- *About 96% of American consumers take part in some way on Mother's Day*
- *Mother's Day is widely reported as the peak day of the year for long distance telephone calls*
- *Mother's Day is the busiest day of the year for many restaurants*
- *Retailers report that Mother's Day is the second highest gift-giving holiday in the United States, second only to Christmas*

On the other hand, Father's Day is seen as just another day. It carries no emotional thrust or emotional involvement whatsoever. There is minimal emphasis or display of honor for Father's Day. Perhaps this is due to father-wounds left unattended or unaddressed. Healing must take place in the lives of men and women with father-wounds.

The presence of the father in the home and in the lives of our children is critical to a healthy America. Father-wounds inflicted during childhood, if not dealt with, can follow that child throughout life. According to the National Fatherhood Initiative's (NFI) Father Facts:

- *Children with involved, loving fathers are significantly more likely to do well in school, have healthy self-esteem, exhibit empathy and pro-social behavior, and avoid high-risk behaviors such as drug use, truancy, and criminal activity compared to children who have uninvolved fathers.*
- *Studies on parent-child relationships and child wellbeing show that a father's love is an important factor in predicting the social, emotional, and cognitive development and functioning of children and young adults.*

Symptoms of a Father-Wound

A **father-wound** is *the injury inflicted on a child who does not sense or receive the affirmation of a father.* This wound is a wound that can be produced intentionally and unintentionally. It is usually an undiagnosed hurt that can remain buried deep within the psyche and the subconscious. It may remain hidden and submerged throughout childhood, and begin to expose itself in the developing stage of young adulthood and beyond. Sufferers of a father-wound are able to live somewhat normal lives, until adverse effects from the wound begin to surface. Then and only then, can the father-wound be acknowledged, addressed, and dealt with.

When father-wounds are not addressed, men may live their lives as a masquerade. This masquerade can cause a man to act as if everything in his life is in order and he has no problems. However, over time the public and private persona may come into conflict. Things may appear fine on the surface and can lead some men to believe that others are the cause of the problems they are facing. Yet, in order for healing to take place, these wounds must be identified.

The symptoms of a father-wound can be displayed in the form of abusiveness or disrespect to others. These symptoms can be manifested physically, emotionally, sexually, verbally, and/or mentally through men who have internalized wounds. According to Kathy Rodriguez, men and boys who carry father-wounds may exemplify some of the following symptoms:

- *Consistently overly defensive about mistakes*
- *Cannot handle criticism*
- *Feeling inferior and insecure as a man*
- *Feeling intimidated in the presence of other men*
- *Overly controlling in order to cover up the feelings of inferiority*
- *Physically or emotionally dependent on the women in your life*
- *In and out of relationships (instability)*
- *Sexually addicted*
- *Chemically addicted*
- *Little or zero emotional connection with others*
- *Abusive and /or disrespectful to others (physical, sexual, verbal, mental, etc.)* [1]

As we look at father-wounds from a male perspective, be honest with yourself and prepare to deal with your wound. As you begin to deal with it, God will usher you into the process of healing, closure, and completeness.

When you have experienced a father-wound, you may develop and encounter feelings of inferiority or insecurity. You may feel that you do not measure up to other men. You may constantly feel as if you have to prove yourself and your manhood. Few men will admit to this sentiment.

Men who have experienced a father-wound may also feel intimidated in the presence of other men. Oftentimes, they may feel as if they do not have as much to offer other men, as other men have to offer them. To compensate for feelings of inadequacy, some men feel the need to subconsciously engage in competition with other men. I assert that men feel this way because they have not been affirmed as a man. These feelings of inferiority and insecurity can produce a sense of intimidation. As in the words of President Barack Obama, *"You are far from disqualified merely because you may have come from a single parent family. You are larger than any statistic and you are inferior to no man."* You may not know your biological father, but if God is on your side, you can achieve anything. Allow the hand of God to nurture, develop, and mature you. Do not allow the absence of your father to anger or frustrate you. Even though it may be painful, choose to become better and to beat the odds.

A man with a father-wound may become controlling, mainly to cover up his sense of inferiority. Many marital issues can be traced back to father-wounds.

Some of the issues that you are facing in your relationship with your spouse may have little or nothing to do with her, but instead, it may be the product of a father-wound. Fathers that are actively involved in their children's lives may try to control and manipulate them, not out of love, but out of the hurt from their own father-wound. These wounds tend to affect those who are closest to you.

Another symptom of a father-wound within males is sexual promiscuity or addiction. Psychologists have suggested that male sexual addicts and deviants are men who have never felt the affirmation of their fathers. This is really a powerful statement. It is hard for most of us to understand how a man is able to go from one woman to the next with no sense of regret or feelings of emotional involvement. Each woman *conquered* becomes just another trophy to put in his case or on his mantle. This type of wounded man has no appreciation for women and zero emotional connectivity to the act of sex. He can experience the act without investing himself emotionally. This type of behavior can be directly traced back to deeply inflicted father-wounds.

For the most part, boys are introduced to sex and sexual promiscuity at an early age. This may have occurred when he happened to look under the seat of a car and found his father or uncle's stash of Playboy or Hustler magazines. As he observed the content contained in these magazines, he internalized what he perceived to be the appropriate sexual emotion. The problem then, as it is now, is that there was no one to share or provide solid counsel and advise him about his sexual behavior. This young boy was never taught that sexual responsibility involves not just the act of sex, but also a level of maturity to properly maintain a relationship. The lack of the father to bring direction or to teach him about sexuality allowed a distorted seed to be planted. This seed is the idea that manhood is solely defined by how many girls he has sex with. He then begins to operate out of the ill-conceived notion that this is the measuring stick by which to measure his manhood. The sad reality is that many adult men still practice this misconception. They boast of having four and five kids all by different women. They are not committing to any of the women and are totally detached from their children. Life is just a game for them. They give no thought or care for the lives of the babies they are producing.

Unfortunately, when young men do not have the presence and advice of a loving father they can receive their definition of manhood from a host of voices. My father drank when he was young. What started as his social drinking became drinking to keep from feeling the pain of dealing with the responsibilities of adulthood. My father believed that drinking proved you were a man. For my father, drinking was one of the measures of manhood from his early teen years. Without someone to validate what it really meant to be a man, he was left to the advice of his "friends". He said this in our interview: *"Four or five of us would go down to the store. We would take turns going in to buy a bottle. Then, we would all sit in the car and drink. Drunk driving wasn't anything then. Everybody in the car had some liquor. That was life. I'm not proud of it, but that was life."*

He continued, *"Alcohol can lead you anywhere. It clouds your mind, just like you're driving in a fog. You think you're happy. It makes you loud and reckless. But the truth is, it isn't doing anything to help you. If you're drinking to solve or avoid the problem, the problem is still there. You're just in darkness. You can have friends who get you into it. But there are lots of kinds of friends. Some will be with you forever, but others won't help you a molecule. Alcohol doesn't do anything for you. It costs. You pay now, and you pay later."*

My father quit drinking years ago, but he still has regrets over losing the things and time that alcohol took from him. How much of that could have been avoided by one word from a loving father? How many lives were affected by his lack of a dad that could tell him that his manhood was not determined by how much he could drink?

Another symptom of a father-wound is being emotionally disconnected. Men who are dealing with a father-wound typically refuse to invest anything in the lives of those around them. They may come home from work, pick up the remote, and spend hours watching the television. They are oblivious to what is going on around them. While his wife deals with all the issues in the home, he is there physically, but detached emotionally from her, the children, and everything else. This type of man thinks as long as he provides financially for his family, everything is fine.

He may tell himself, "I bring home the money, so I've done my part." As mature men, we must understand the multi-dimensional aspect of being a husband and a father. Fathers realize that just paying the bills is no longer good enough. They understand the importance of being emotionally invested in the lives of their wives and children.

While it is true that provision involves the material aspects, such as shelter, food, and clothing, a good father also provides for spiritual and emotional needs. It is not enough just 'being around' your children. You have to *be in their world*. You need to connect to them where they are. What is *important* to them should be *important* to you.

God desires to bring healing and restoration to your life. He is not interested in shaming or condemning you. As men, we have been dealing with emotional wounds created by our fathers in secrecy and have been in pain far too long. Now is the time to deal with the wound and walk in liberty, so that you can pursue your destiny and life-long dreams. You do not have to live a double life, but as you deal with the root of your issues, you can conquer and silence the curse resulting from your father-wound.

Chapter One: Discussion Questions

- How have you been impacted by a father-wound?

- Have you exhibited any symptoms of a father-wound?

- In what way could you show more honor to your father?

- What hinders you from showing honor to your father?

Chapter Two

THE POWER OF AFFIRMATION

Nothing I've ever done has given me more joys and rewards than being a father to my children.

~Bill Cosby

And lo a voice from heaven, saying, This is My beloved Son, in whom I am well pleased.

Matthew 3:17

Father-wounds are caused by the lack of affirmation. Being affirmed and validated is vital to our emotional development. Affirmation of our peers, our friends, our co-workers, and of those we are in relationship with is needed, yet there is nothing as powerful as the affirmation of a father. The word **affirmation** in Latin means to *make firm*. An affirmation is like a declaration. It is a series of positive words repeated over and over again that will eventually come in line with a visual concept. Affirmation is a creative force in the life of a child. When the power of the affirmation of a father is released, the putty-like substance in the subconscious mind of the child becomes set-firm and established with positive thoughts and mindsets. The subconscious mind is like a piece of clay that can be impressed. This putty-like substance makes up the subconscious areas of the mind. Affirmation, when used with wisdom, remolds and solidifies the subconscious identity of the child. It stabilizes the child's thought patterns and mentally alters the mood of that child, until thoughts and actions are changed into affirmations. This opens the mind of the child to new possibilities and unexpected creative sources.

When someone has not been affirmed by their father, they may become fragile. Without the affirmation of a father, a child can be uncertain and defenseless in the face of life's issues. If they have not been affirmed with the fact that they are strong, they may see themselves as weak. Fear and thoughts of the unknown can also hold them captive. They may find themselves in a precarious position when dealing with and in relationship with others, because they were not empowered in their first relationships in life. Their concept of fatherhood may be tenuous at best. They have not been told they are strong and capable to handle the turmoil of life, so they are at a disadvantage. They are vulnerable to others, and at times, taken advantage of easily.

> *And Isaac loved Esau, because he did eat of his venison: but Rebekah loved Jacob.*
>
> *Genesis 25:28*

Affirmation is powerful. In Genesis 25:28, we see that Isaac loves Esau and Rebecca loves Jacob. Therefore, for Jacob, all of his life, there was an undertone of rejection – *a father-wound.* Since there was a realm of rejection in Jacob's life, there seemed to be nothing he could do to get the affirmation he desired from his father, Isaac. However, his mother Rebecca loved him. Please understand this: A woman is not able to affirm a man suitably. She can encourage him, she can speak into him, but she cannot affirm him.

Rebecca knew the importance of the blessing from the father. When she heard that Isaac was getting ready to bless Esau, look at her actions. She pulled Jacob aside and she covered him in Esau's garments. She allowed the aroma of Esau's clothes to be on him, and then she prepared the meal for him to present to his father, Isaac. Through deception, she arranged it so that when Jacob went into the presence of Isaac, Isaac would think that he was Esau. She did all of this because she understood the significance of the father's blessing. Affirmation (the blessing) of the father was so imperative that Rebecca was willing to use trickery to ensure Jacob received it. She knew that if she could get him into the presence of his father, he would receive a generational blessing. He would not have to walk through life cursed without the father's blessing, but he could walk with the honor connected to the affirmed blessing.

Gordon Dalbey, in an article entitled, "*Father Hunger*", refers to a statement made by an editor whose father had recently died, saying, "I'm still waiting for my father to talk to me about sex and success. I'm still waiting for him to talk to me about money and marriage. I'm still waiting for my father to talk to me about religion and raising kids." He went on to say, "The shame of it is that I do not know a man my age who does not feel like he's navigating his life without a map!"[2] Even though this editor has experienced great success in his life, his statement speaks volumes. We do not sense that his father was abusive, yet, for whatever reasons, he did not release affirmation verbally into his son. His lack of direction is noted, even though this son has achieved success professionally. He also noted that this is not an isolated thought. This editor is going through his life feeling lost and clearly at a disadvantage. One might ask what the disadvantage is. The disadvantage is that he had to navigate the turbulence of life without the father's voice to affirm and to speak into his life's issues. He not only navigated through life without a map, but he was not affirmed and solidified internally. That's a lonely walk! No affirmation, no direction, and no guidance. Sad to say, most men fully understand and can relate to his statement.

> *For what man knows the things of a man except the spirit of the man which is in him?*
>
> *1 Corinthians 2:11(NKJV)*

I am a product of a single-parent family. My mother, Marie B. Banks, raised me. I am who I am today because of the powerful and strong woman who influenced my life. By no means would I ever dishonor my mother or any other woman in my life. I will always honor my awesome mother. As a child, I was shaped and nurtured by her. Nothing can remotely compare to a mother's love and support. I'm married to a powerful woman who walks with me as my kingdom partner; not behind me, not in front of me, but beside me. She is my equal. I'm not greater than her, nor is she greater than me. I'm not her superior, nor is she my superior. We understand that the commanded blessing was pronounced on both Adam ***and*** Eve (Gen. 1:26). There are women of great power and influence in my life, over my life, before me, beside me, and even my daughter coming behind me.

Even though I have been blessed to have such dynamic women in my life, only a man can impart some things into a son. In *Parade Magazine*, June 21, 2009, Barack Obama wrote, "In many ways, I came to understand the importance of fatherhood through its absence—both in my life and in the lives of others. I came to understand that the hole a man leaves when he abandons his responsibility to his children is one that no government can fill. We can do everything possible to provide good jobs and good schools and safe streets for our kids, but it will never be enough to fully make up the difference."[3]

Effects of Affirmation

> *And Jesus, when he was baptized, went up straightway out of the water: and, lo, the heavens were opened unto him, and he saw the Spirit of God descending like a dove, and lighting upon him: And lo a voice from heaven, saying, This is my beloved Son, in whom I am well pleased.*
>
> *Matthew 3:16-17*

Look at what happens in this encounter of affirmation. The Father is speaking over The Son. The blessing is being released through the spoken word. The source of the blessing is The Father.

Father means *one with authority; teacher*. A father is one who opens his children to new realms and new dimensions of experiment and growth that brings true maturity. Fathers are equipped with the ability and power to pronounce a thing over the lives of their sons and daughters, and they will operate in it. When a father affirms, he speaks purpose, he speaks encouragement, he speaks identity, and he speaks strength. **Through affirmation, identity is released:** *This is* *my son* (Matthew 3:17). **Self-confidence is also released:** *In whom I am well pleased.* When our sons and daughters are affirmed, they will know who they are and will display an unprecedented level of security and self-confidence.

Self-confidence is a character trait that is displayed throughout life. Nowhere is it more evident than in sports. Tiger Woods, the first athlete to reach a billion dollars in earnings according to Forbes.com[4], is the wealthiest athlete in the world. From the beginning, his love for the sport of golf was guided, nurtured, managed, and inspired by his father, Earl Woods. On September 3, 2006, in an interview with Ed Bradley on 60 Minutes, Tiger said his father played a tremendous role in shaping him, "*He's my best friend. And you know, having your best friend be your father is a very unique thing,*" he said. When he needed help competing against older, stronger boys, Tiger turned to his father and his special forces training. "*I came to dad. I said, 'Dad, can you make me tough?*' He said, "'*Yeah, and you're not going to like it. Are you willing to go through it?'And I said, 'Yeah,'*" Tiger recalls. *"And he would get in my grill. He'd really make you feel insignificant. And then he'd get to the point, the line - he'd never cross it, and back off. And then he'd keep pushing the next time, and it wasn't as far. And eventually, I looked at him and smiled, and [said] 'What are you trying to do here?'And he said, 'All right, you're done."* The bond between Tiger and his father was remarkable and noteworthy. They shared a relationship that all fathers could pattern themselves after.

Another father/son relationship that promoted self-confidence is that of Kobe Bryant and his father Joe "Jellybean" Bryant, who was a professional basketball player himself. When Joe was not traveling with his team, he spent time playing sports with his children. Kobe showed skill and talent in sports at a very young age. He adored his father. Bryant said in the New York Times, "My father's my best friend." The bond developed at an early age between Kobe and his father has proven to be instrumental in Kobe becoming the superstar athlete he is today.

Tiger and Kobe are going to progress to where they too will become greater people than they are athletes. It is a natural healthy progression. Right now, it is just about winning the Masters, US Open, or another championship. I believe, as they mature, and we're all maturing, these particular athletes will capitalize on their influence, transcend athletics, and make a global impact transforming the lives of others. Muhammad Ali understood that power of transcending his athletic ability. He is still the most recognizable and celebrated athlete in the world. It is universally understood that Muhammad Ali is not just a great athlete, but that he is a great human being.

Even though I have never played tennis, Arthur Ashe has always been one of my greatest heroes. I saw something in him. Even though I do not understand the game of tennis, I saw that something in him transcended the sport. The tennis courts or winning Wimbledon did not define him. The impact Arthur Ashe had over my life speaks volumes. I read his book, "*The Days of Grace*", many times. Arthur Ashe had such an impact on my life that when he died I took off work to go to his funeral. He was someone who had such a tremendous impact on the lives of others, because he gave so much of himself while he lived. Even though he has passed on, he is still making an impartation into the generations after him. He too made great contributions to humanity.

At the same time, I am deeply concerned about those with influence who have not dealt with their own father-wounds. They are living out of their pain and anger. This agony and despair is becoming more profound and pronounced at a younger age.

However, not all father/son relationships can be seen as positive and nurturing. Tyler Perry, the highly successful director, producer, author, and movie star, recently exposed the physical and emotional abuse that he endured as a child from the hands of his own father. After viewing a screening of the new movie *Precious*, in which a teenage girl is struggling to overcome mental and physical abuse, Tyler Perry said, "*A large part of my childhood had just played out before my eyes. I always thought I would die before I grew up*," Perry wrote in a letter to fans on his website before recounting the various abuses he suffered.

Perry said that his father once beat him so badly with an extension cord that the skin came off his back. He said that his father hated that he was sickly, liked to read, write, and draw. His father also hated that he was darker-skinned; "*He didn't think he could make a dark baby. He just hated everything about me I guess.*" Perry said, "*Watching* Precious *hit me so hard. I sat there in tears realizing that somehow, by the grace of God, I made it through. My tears were tears of joy, being thankful that I made it.*

"To know that the little boy that I was went through all that - he went through and made it. Then me, as a man... I have to take on the responsibility of forgiving all of those people. I owe it to that little boy that

I was and, more than that, I owe it to the man that I am. Think about it, as a child we have no recourse. We have nowhere to go. We have to endure it. But as adults, we have choices. I choose to forgive with all my might. Forgiveness has been my weapon of choice. It has helped to free me."

Another well-known athlete who appears to have suffered from a father-wound is Michael Vick. Vick, one of the highest paid celebrity NFL players, was recently released after serving a short prison term. He is the product of teenage parents who raised him in the projects. His father was not a positive influence on him growing up. This successful and popular quarterback, recently reinstated as a pro ballplayer, has found redemption in a father figure by the name of Coach Tony Dungy. Coach Dungy has taken on the very public role of fathering, mentoring, and supporting this "son". Their relationship is a tangible display of the restoration of the father-son relationship that is vital in the formation of social and emotional development, even in the life of a mature adult.

Coach Dungy, a humble man of faith, is the first African American head coach to win a Super Bowl. He is the product of a stable middle-class two parent home. He is also a retired coach and bestselling author of inspirational books, such as "*Quiet Strength.*" He is a mentor and father figure to many of his former players, young men in prison, and their families. His name was also recently submitted as a potential candidate for the title "Fatherhood Czar," under the President Obama administration.

What is so uncommon about Vick and Dungy is that they were raised in very different environments, but they now find themselves in a sincere father-son relationship. In a Wall Street Journal article when discussing the environment that Vick grew up in, Coach Dungy stated, "For so many of these young people growing up nowadays, seeing it (drugs and dog fighting) on the streets, seeing it around, it's not like it's so scary to them as it is for us. It is part of the way they grew up. It's an educational process that we can sometimes take for granted; well everyone should know that, nobody should get involved with that. But they've done it. And I think that was Mike's case. The dog-fighting culture is something I haven't seen, but it wasn't foreign to him." Coach Dungy went on to further state that "Michael Vick resonates with young people." He also added that in all his years of prison ministry and coaching, he has seen the impact of the breakdown of families, with all the missing dads, especially among his players.

Michael Vick has acknowledged his actions and has realized the need for a father in his own children's lives. Vick stated, "I really miss my three kids who are growing up without their father. I feel I was given a chance to be a role model and I blew it." However, I believe God is a God of second chances and we are rooting for Michael Vick's future success as a great athlete, and more importantly a great father!

The Hip-Hop Culture: A Fatherless Genre

One phenomenon taking popular culture by storm is the "*hip-hop*" or "*rap*" culture. It is not just a musical genre, but it is a fatherless genre void of the influence of fathers. The hip-hop and rap music culture is a reflection of the dominant culture in America. It is also shaping and molding the culture at the same time. In the lyrics of many hip-hop and rap songs, we hear many unacceptable and degrading references that exploit women with sex and drugs. It is filled with violence and fueled by anger. This stems from the lack of fathers available to speak into the lives of these artists. If there were an affirming father present, he would tell his son that it is inappropriate to speak of women in such a debasing, demeaning, and shameful manner. He would remind his son that he was born of a woman, and should not talk about any mother, sister, or daughter in such a degrading way.

Many fathers have not been fathered, and are learning the art of fathering as they go along. On June 15, 2008, Barak Obama delivered a Father's day Speech at The Apostolic Church of God in Chicago, Illinois. He said, "*It's up to us, as fathers and parents, to instill this ethic of excellence in our children. It's up to us to say to our daughters, don't ever let images on TV tell you what you are worth, because I expect you to dream without limit and reach for those goals. It's up to us to tell our sons, those songs on the radio may glorify violence, but in my house we give glory to achievement, self-respect, and hard work. It's up to us to set these high expectations. And that means meeting these expectations ourselves. That means setting examples of excellence in our own lives.*"

In that same speech, President Obama also said, "*Yes we need more cops on the street. Yes, we need fewer guns in the hands of people who shouldn't have them. Yes, we need more money for our schools, and more outstanding teachers in the classroom, and more afterschool programs for our children. Yes, we need more jobs, and more job training, and more opportunity in our communities. But we also need families to raise our children.*"[5]

Missing-In-Action

Too many fathers have abandoned their responsibilities by being absent from the lives of their children. Just because you have the seed, the ability to produce a child does not make you a father. Fatherhood is more than biology. It is a development of your character, of your mind, and of your heart. When you develop as a father, you begin to understand that your masculinity and fatherhood is not based upon the number of children you have, but on how you are providing for your sons and daughters. If you are man enough to have them conceived by a woman, then you have to be man enough to take care of them and invest yourself in them. Forty-eight percent of all black children live without fathers in their homes. Too many fathers are missing in action (MIA) – missing from too many lives and too many homes.

It is important that we actively engage in the lives of our children. There's a pain that a child feels when he goes to catch the bus on the first day of school, and there's no father there to wave him off. There's a pain in the heart of the young boy who scores his first touchdown and his father is not there to celebrate this milestone in his life. There's a pain in the heart of the son who shoots the winning basket of the basketball game and his daddy is not there to say, "That's my boy! You did it!" There's a pain when a little boy matriculates through elementary school, middle school, high school, and college and he walks across the stage to receive his diploma, but there's no father to embrace him and say "Son, I'm proud of you." There's a father-wound, because no affirmation is provided to this child from his father.

In courtrooms, we often see sons facing judges with no fathers present for support. This is a sad commentary. This child is facing a sentence that will affect the rest of his life and all you find, for the most part, is the mother there in the courtroom. You do not see the fathers. Where are the uncles? Where are the deacons? Where are the elders? Where are the leaders? I have been to many courtrooms as a minister and on many occasions, I have been the only male present, except for the judge and the bailiff. When a male shows up in support of the accused son, the courts seem to deal with that son differently than one who has no male support present.

When a father is involved in the life of his son, it is less likely that his son will ever end up facing a judge. Real fathers lead and guide their sons in the right direction. They instill in them the value of working an honest job, even if the pay is minimum wage. Fathers are able to explain to their sons the consequences of illegal acts. The effects of a father's absence are profound, as evidenced by the following statistics.

- 51 percent of children raised by unmarried mothers are raised in poverty

- 69 percent of all black children are born to single mothers

- 48 percent of all black children live without fathers in their homes

- 85 percent of all children that exhibit behavioral disorders come from fatherless homes

- 71 percent of all high school drop outs come from fatherless homes

- 70-80 percent of juveniles in state operated institutions come from fatherless homes

- 85 percent of all youths sitting in prison grew up in a fatherless home

Additionally, the lack of a father's presence affects a child's education and behavior. Nothing can substitute for the presence of a father. Things may not have worked out between you and the mother of your child, and the relationship may have ended in divorce, but as a father, it is imperative that you do not sever your relationship with your child. You have to be more than a sperm donor. You have to invest in the destiny of your sons and your daughters. Children with absent fathers are at risk of the following:

- ***More likely to live in poverty.*** *Source: U.S. Census Bureau, Children's Living Arrangements and Characteristics: March 2002, P200-547, Table C8. Washington D.C.: GPO, 2003.*
- ***More likely to be incarcerated as juveniles.*** *Source: Harper, Cynthia C. and Sara S. McLanahan. "Father Absence and Youth Incarceration." Journal of Research on Adolescence 14 (September 2004): 369-397.*
- ***More likely to be incarcerated as adults.*** *Source: Snell, Tracy L and Danielle C. Morton. Women in Prison: Survey of Prison Inmates, 1991. Bureau of Justice Statistics Special Report. Washington, DC: US Department of Justice, 1994: 4.*

- ***More likely to use illegal substances.*** *Source: Hoffmann, John P. "The Community Context of Family Structure and Adolescent Drug Use." Journal of Marriage and Family 64 (May 2002): 314-330.*
- ***Twice as likely to experience physical abuse, emotional abuse, or educational neglect.*** *Source: America's Children: Key National Indicators of Well-Being. Table SPECIAL1. Washington, D.C.: Federal Interagency Forum on Child and Family Statistics, 1997.*
- ***Twice as likely to drop out of school. Source:*** *U.S. Department of Health and Human Services. National Center for Health Statistics. Survey on Child Health. Washington, D.C.: GPO, 1993.*
- ***Twice as likely to repeat a grade. Source:*** *Nord, Christine Winquist, and Jerry West. Fathers' and Mothers' Involvement in Their Children's Schools by Family Type and Resident Status. (NCES 2001-032). Washington, D.C.: U.S. Department of Education, National Center for Education Statistics, 2001.*

We need fathers in our lives that we can honor, receive counsel from, and with whom we can share life's challenges. Even though a father is definitely needed in the early years of a child's life, their presence is needed just as much, if not more so, in the lives of grown men. You never get to the point where you become so grown that you do not need the voice and the affirmation of a father in your life. How can I be the husband I need to be? Whom can I talk to about the challenges of raising my children? Who can counsel me on my financial situation? A father should provide his son with answers to these questions.

Financial and Emotional Responsibility

Every father has a legal responsibility to support his children. In addition to financial support, you are equally accountable for spending quality time with them. I believe that the day will come in the judicial system when judges will not just assign monetary amounts of child support, but they will also require fathers to invest a specified amount of time into their children. If only financial support is provided, the father is nothing more than a financier.

When parents do not invest time in their sons and daughters, the children grow up with massive voids in their lives. You cannot be a silent partner in their lives. It is not enough just to be there for your children physically. That is important, but it is equally important to be there for them emotionally. You have to be emotionally, mentally, and spiritually connected to your sons and daughters. When they cry, you should be right there crying with them. When they celebrate, you should be right there celebrating with them.

Fatherhood is something that we are continually growing into. It is important as fathers to experience your child's world. We tend to bring children into our world, but how often, as fathers, do we go into theirs? God corrected me personally concerning this. He showed me that I had been attending my son's basketball games physically, but I was mentally detached from my son's game. Throughout the game, I had my cell phone out and was busy texting. What kind of message was this sending my son? I was sending him a mixed message at best, that impressed upon him that I might be there physically, yet absent emotionally. From that point on, I made a commitment that I may not attend every game, but those that I do attend, I will be there fully engaged – all of me, with the cell phone turned off.

Time Matters

A young successful attorney said: "The greatest gift I ever received was a gift I got one Christmas when my dad gave me a small box. Inside was a note saying, "Son, this year I will give you 365 hours, an hour every day after dinner. It's yours. We'll talk about what you want to talk about, we'll go where you want to go, play what you want to play. It will be your hour!" My dad not only kept his promise, he said, but every year he renewed it- and it's the greatest gift I ever had in my life. I am the result of his time."

- Moody Monthly

I recall a situation with my daughter where she was seeking the Lord on a particular issue. She discussed the issue with my wife and I, yet we still had not gained an understanding or clarity on the matter. While I was in Detroit, Michigan preparing for a television interview that would air all over the world, I received a call from my wife. She shared with me her thoughts about our daughter and it came down to me having to make a decision. I spoke to my daughter and I said to her, "Baby, I'm standing with you," but I was still unsettled. Here I am in Detroit, hundreds of miles away, getting ready to speak to an international audience, and my daughter is at home struggling with a situation. I said to my wife, "Honey, I'll call you right back." I hung up and immediately called the producers from the TV station and I said, "I need a release from the TV appearance. I need to get back home. My daughter needs her father right now. I thank God for the opportunity, but I just can't do it at this time." Yes, I am Bishop, but at home, I am Daddy, and I must avail myself to be there for my children whenever they need me.

Fathers, your family must always be your primary responsibility. How many of us have allowed job opportunities to pull us away from our family? Your focus should not only be on your business, your education, or on your call to preach, but primarily on taking care of your home. If you cannot take care of your home, then you do not need to be leading anything. You have to make sure that your house is in order first. What does it profit you to gain the whole world and to lose those who are dearest to you? Make a declaration, "As for me and my house, we're going to get it right!"

An Epidemic of Fatherlessness

> *For though ye have ten thousand instructors in Christ, yet have ye not many fathers: for in Christ Jesus I have begotten you through the gospel.*
>
> *I Corinthians 4:15*

In this nation and in this world, many are being raised in single parent homes – mostly by single parent mothers. This epidemic has seemingly become the 'norm' for the times we are living in. While we definitely applaud and honor all single parents who are raising their children, sometimes even without any assistance or financial support, we especially applaud those who are raising mighty men and women of God who do not continue to perpetuate the same ills of our society. We wholeheartedly thank God for the mothers who have single handedly raised their children, but this should not be so. The time has come for this to change. Fathers must now decide to take their rightful place in the lives of their sons and daughters. Fathers must now own up to their responsibility to actively nurture and raise their children.

> *As arrows are in the hand of a mighty man, so are children of the youth.*
>
> *Psalm 127:4*

Children are an extension of our lives. As fathers, we are to live our lives in a way that is acceptable for our children to follow. We are to guide and release our sons and daughters, just like arrows, ensuring they hit the mark of their destiny. This is accomplished through teaching, training, giving directions, and the power of affirmation. The sad commentary is that many of our children have not been raised with this kind of upbringing. Many of our children have not been fathered, so they are growing up yearning for direction and gravitating towards whatever comes along. If the father was present to provide guidance, it is highly likely that the children would not venture far from the mark.

> *Train up a child in the way he should go: and when he is old, he will not depart from it.*
>
> *Proverbs 22:6*

Why will they not depart? Because they have been targeted,

trained, and affirmed. If we do not deal with the lack of a father's guidance, the cycle will continue throughout generations and the pain of it will not cease. There are grown men and women who are still dealing with the pain caused by father-wounds. The Good News is that because you are willing and ready to do what is necessary to break this cycle, the iniquities of the fathers will not be passed on to the successive generations.

From One Generation to the Next

With each generation, we are progressing and advancing. Our grandfather's generation simply provided financially. Often, they had to move or relocate for jobs, but they would send money back home to ensure the needs of their families were met. Our fathers, for the most part, lived with their children in the same home. They provided the physical presence, but in many cases, they were not there emotionally. Let this generation, our generation, be the one that provides support financially, physically, and emotionally. Let this generation be the generation that will bestow spiritual impartation to our children. We understand our obligation to raise our sons and daughters in the fear and the admonition of our Lord. We know and understand that we need to cover our children and to walk with them. The enemy is trying to come up against our commitment to break addictions and cycles in our lives. Men, I want you to know that God is going to bless you to be that affirmative father to your sons and daughters that is so vital in this day and hour. As you open your heart and stand firm on His Word, God will bring healing to all your father-wounds.

What are the first steps toward healing father-wounds?

- *Acknowledge the fact that you have a father.*

Several years ago, my brother Bruce shared with me that he recognized the need to have his father in his life. There will be times in your life where you will recognize the need of another man. There is nothing unusual or strange about needing another man to sow wisdom or counsel into your life. It is normal and healthy to need other men and to display love towards your sons.

- *Allow the process to begin.*

The process of healing will take time; however, it starts with you getting your mind and thoughts in order. Your father may have wounded you. His actions may have hurt you, but you have to be willing to let the painful thoughts and memories go. You must be willing to allow God to take control of your thoughts and emotions. You have to be willing to go into the process with an open mind and an open heart, even though you do not know what the outcome will be. For some, it may lead to reconciliation or reconnection with your father. For others, the attempt to reconcile or reconnect may fail, but when you prepare yourself emotionally and spiritually, God will allow healing to take place, regardless of the outcome.

- *Surround yourself with godly men.*

As you are going through the healing process, make sure that you surround yourself with other healthy men that are maturing in the things of God. Keep company with men who desire to be what God is calling them to be. These men will help you develop in your fatherhood.

Chapter Two: **Discussion Questions**

- What does self-confidence mean to you? Do you exemplify the traits of self-confidence?

- Who is your role model?

- Why have you chosen this person to be your role model?

Chapter Three

FATHERS AND DAUGHTERS

"Before I had Ming, there was nothing greater than me. I cared only about myself. Now I'd lie in the box and close the lid for my daughters. I never thought I'd say that."

~Russell Simmons

It is the father's responsibility to affirm his daughter and to make her solid and strong. He must speak into her life continually and affirm that she is special. Even Jesus Himself received affirmation from His Father.

And suddenly a voice came from heaven, saying "This is my beloved Son, in whom I am well pleased.

Matthew 3:17(NKJV)

A daughter, who has not been affirmed by her father, even though she may not be able to articulate it, knows that something is missing in her life. Her mother will do everything she can do for her. She can dress her up, style her hair, paint her nails, adorn her in jewels, and instruct her in the ways of a woman. However, it is the father's voice that is assigned to speak over her and to affirm her as a woman. A daughter gets her ideas and assurance of her femininity when she hears affirmation from her father and when she obtains his favor. When she does not get affirmation from her father, she will hunger for it and seek to obtain it from others. According to Kathy Rodriguez, women lacking affirmation exhibit many symptoms, such as:

- *Feeling insecure as a woman*
- Being *clingy and over dependent on others*
- *Overcompensating in relationships*
- *Seeking male attention and approval*
- *Being high maintenance*
- *Being demanding*
- *Being manipulative*
- *Developing a history of relationships with under-functioning and/or controlling men*
- *Displacing anger*
- *Showing hatred towards men*
- *Creating unhealthy attachments to un-attachable people*
- *Living in a fantasy world*

These symptoms are the result of a father-wound. There is a hole within the heart of a young woman who has been wounded by her father. She subconsciously senses the need for a father to affirm her and when that voice is absent; she becomes vulnerable and is often taken advantage of by anyone who comes along. She may constantly seek male attention and approval, or she may pursue relations with someone much older. It may not be because she truly loves that older person, but she may be seeking a fatherly-type affirmation to acknowledge her worth.

Just Affirm Her

Fathers, it is very likely that your daughter will not be anything like your son. She will be someone outside of the realm of your understanding, but you are still called to cover, protect, and provide for her.

Discriminatory religious traditions and social norms are broken when you bring affirmation to your daughters. Society has told us that women are not important and that they are inferior, but we know this is not true. God is no respecter of persons and we shouldn't be either. He is able to use them just as he used Deborah (Read the book of Judges, Chapters 4 and 5).

Like Deborah, you can become a wife, a mother, a prophetess, and a judge. According to my wife, Dr. Keira Taylor-Banks, author of *The Matriarchal Dimension*, "Deborah was extraordinarily multifaceted. And so are the vast majority of anointed women – we are multi-dimensional in the sense that we are not limited to one assignment, but women are packing with gifting that often remains suppressed and underdeveloped. Rather than being summoned to battle, women are left on the sidelines never fully enabled to release our full arsenal of gifting."[6] However, gender is no barrier whatsoever to what God desires to do in you. If an African American male can get into the White House, surely we can declare the same future for our daughters. It is no longer impossible or a foreign concept to daughters who have had this affirmed and declared over their lives. There are no limits to what you can attain. You have been equipped to perform anything that you desire to do. You do not have to wait for a knight in shining armor to come along to take care of you. You are already complete before you arrive at the altar. You can be single and still be anointed and blessed of God. God has validated you and has accepted you just as you are. You have been created just as He has planned. Daughter, you can reach your destiny.

I will praise thee; for I am fearfully and wonderfully made:

Psalm 139:14

There is something I've recently noticed in very successful women in all walks of life, but especially in the black community. This observation has made a distinct impression in my mind. I have noticed that sharp, affluent, and smart women are choosing not to marry. What has happened in their hearts that has caused them to come to the decision not to marry? Could this be a cry or a statement that they have been deeply hurt and wounded by a father? Could it be because they saw their mothers go through so much heartache that they believe they are better off remaining unmarried? It is not always that they do not like men or do not have a desire to marry; many times, it is the pain of the father-wound they carry within that is too severe.

A Father-Wound at the Well

On the other hand, you may find women who have been so wounded that they continually seek out validation through relationships. They will marry repeatedly in search of affirmation. The biblical story known as the woman at the well is a prime example.

> *Then saith the woman of Samaria unto him, How is it that thou, being a Jew, askest drink of me, which am a woman of Samaria? for the Jews have no dealings with the Samaritans. Jesus answered and said unto her, "If thou knewest the gift of God, and who it is that saith to thee, Give me to drink; thou wouldest have asked of him, and he would have given thee living water". The woman saith unto him, Sir, thou hast nothing to draw with, and the well is deep: from whence then hast thou that living water? Art thou greater than our father Jacob,..., Jesus answered and said unto her, "Whosoever drinketh of this water shall thirst again: But whosoever drinketh of the water that I shall give him shall never thirst; John 4: 9-14*

A little later in the conversation between Jesus and the Samaritan woman:

> *Jesus saith unto her, "Go, call thy husband, and come hither." The woman answered and said, "I have no husband" Jesus said unto her, "Thou hast well said, I have no husband: For thou hast had five husbands; and he who thou now hast is not thy husband: in that saidst thou truly." The woman saith unto him, Sir, I perceive that thou art a prophet'.*
>
> *John 4: 16-19*

This woman of Samaria had an encounter with Jesus at the well. I believe this woman was suffering from a father-wound. How else could she marry so many times and even feel the need to have a man in her life that was not hers? She exhibited so many of the symptoms I have asserted here.

This Samaritan woman had five husbands and was now with a sixth man that was not her husband. She marveled that Jesus knew so much about her personal life. She had never met a man who knew her like this. She did not realize she needed to be made whole, until that 'seventh' man arrived on the scene and into her life. Jesus was that 'seventh' man. By His affirmation, she was made whole. Biblically, the number seven represents completion. Because of this 'seventh' man, who spoke into her life, she became whole and complete. She received what she needed from this 'seventh man', who was "living water" and a well of renewal and restoration.

Yes Daughter, I Am Talking To You

Daughters, some of you who are reading this book are receiving these words as a father's affirmation. This book is serving as the father's voice that you needed. Maybe your father is no longer alive or has never been present in your life. For this reason, you have lived your life with a void in your heart. You have been longing for and waiting to have this emptiness in your heart filled. There are some things that only a father can release into the life of a daughter, and this book is bringing that affirmation and healing to some of you at this very moment.

As a father, I speak over your life that you can walk in your overflow right now. You can go to law school and become a lawyer if that is your desire. You can be a doctor if that is what you want to do. Even if there are things that they say a woman cannot do, if God is on your side, your gender cannot hold you back. Some women may say, "I have attended school, received my degree, and I am still getting paid less than a man." If this is the case, I would encourage you to open your own business! Go after your dreams and pursue your destiny! Whatever you put your hands to do shall prosper, daughter, so give no attention to what society says you can or cannot do. You have the Kingdom anointing over your life, which empowers you to succeed and transcend limitations.

Daughters, in the absence of fathers, you have been surrounded by uncles, brothers, and neighbors who have affirmed that you are the apple of God's eye. You have been surrounded by great women who are able to assure you that with God, nothing is impossible for you! You are living in your finest hour! In this hour, Heaven is pregnant with possibilities for women!

God is breaking the box of what you may have thought was a male society. God is going to release teenagers and women to do things they have never done before. God is releasing women into corporations, into businesses, into Wall Street, and yes, even into politics. God says to you daughter that He will be your friend, your father, your mother, your brother, and your sister in this hour. Everything that you need, the God who is the "*I AM*" will supernaturally download it into your life.

Mothers, you may be divorced from the father of your child, but whatever the status, it is important that you do not block him from her life. He still has the right to be actively involved in her life. Whatever has happened between the two of you, keep it between the two of you. Do not use the child as a pawn to take advantage, manipulate, or try to control the situation. The relationship may not have worked out, but it is imperative that as a mother, you do everything in your power to safeguard your daughter's relationship with her father. She needs her father to be involved in her life. She needs him to affirm her. Understand that she is his daughter, a product of his seed, and she needs him. His presence is vital to her health and emotional well-being.

Healthy Father and Daughter Relationships

The relationship developed between a daughter and her father will be the prototype she will use to develop future male/female relationships. In a healthy father and daughter relationship, the daughter grows up with the sense that her father does affirm her. She grows up knowing that she is celebrated and safe in her relationship with her father. She feels protected and cherished by her father and knows she can open herself to him without the fear of being violated or betrayed. She trusts him and feels whole and complete in his presence. It is a totally non-threatening and non-sexual type of relationship where she has connected wholeheartedly with her father.

As fathers, our role in the lives of our daughters is bigger than being the disciplinarian or just the financial provider. We have an instrumental role to play in every stage of their life – when they are born, when they are toddlers, when they are teenagers, and when they become young adults. The most critical role is to affirm them, to assure them, and reinforce to them that they can be and do whatever they desire to do, and that nothing is impossible to them.

She is looking for you to be there to speak vision and direction into her dreams and ideas. She is looking to you for guidance, as she develops socially and intellectually. As a father, you can impart wisdom into your daughters just as you do with your sons. You can help her understand that God is doing great things in and through her. She has full and rightful authority to enter into any realm that she desires. There is no job that is excluded from her and no possibility beyond her reach because of her gender. As a young woman, she needs to know that her value is not based upon her physical body, but that she carries much depth, creative energy, and genius on the inside. She has much power and intellectual influence.

The words and actions of fathers cultivate, shape, and mold their daughters. It is important that we speak the things that they need to hear from us. We cannot allow ourselves to be the fathers that do not give the needed affirmation to our daughters.

One day I asked my daughter, Keira Iman, what a father meant to her. I said, "Honey, what is a father to you?" She replied, "A provider." I laughed and said, "I know that's right." Then she went on to share how she saw a father as "the provider." She said, he is not just a provider financially, but she saw a father as a '*problem solver.*'

She saw a father as a '*disciplinarian*', a '*protector*', and someone who *brings confirmation to her about what God is saying*. She said a father is a '*guiding hand*.' She even stated that she saw a father as a '*crisis manager*.' For example, if her car breaks down, her father would know what to do. She went on to say that a father to her is the '*bridge between the mother and the daughter*.' Isn't it amazing? We have to be a '*provider*' and much more to them. We have to be the role model. Our daughters need to see that although daddy may not wash the dishes a lot, he is responsible for other things in the home. They need to observe the equality in the relationship between the father and the mother. They have to know that they are not restricted by the roles that the father and mother play.

During my time with Rev. Dr. James R. Taylor, whom I affectionately refer to as Pop Taylor, I discovered a man who takes great pride in being able to exemplify true manhood before his children. Pop Taylor raised three wonderful daughters, including my very own wife Keira. He told me that first and foremost, he wanted to be an example to his daughters. And that as a good example of a man, he had to treat their mother the way they should be treated.

Later in my conversation with Pop Taylor, I asked him to share the legacy he desires to leave to his three daughters. He answered, *"Take care of your kids. Educate your kids so they have opportunities and get a good job. And then teach them how to be independent. Stand by your husband. Treat people right. Try to do the right thing. We're not perfect, but be as perfect as you can be. Be honest. My grandmother used to say, tell the truth if it kills you. And above and beyond all, love each other. Be faithful to each other to the end."*

Chapter Three: Discussion Questions

- What words of affirmation have been spoken into your life by your father or a father-figure?

- What symptoms do you exhibit from lack of affirmation?

- When was the last time that you spoke affirmation to your daughter. And what did you say?

Chapter Four

FATHERLESS DAUGHTERS

Nothing can replace the voice of a father in the life of his daughter; it is her lifeline to who she really is.

~Deborah G. Hunter

As a man attempting to address and discuss a serious topic like the father-wound, I realize that there is a lot of ground to cover. I believe the desired healing is not contingent on just the **seed** or the words that are being released, but hinges more so on the condition of the **soil**.

The **seed** is the truth and the **soil** refers to the heart and the mind. This message is being released to hearts that are willing to receive the truth and to minds that are open to the possibility of change and forgiveness. Mindsets will be broken when you are able to understand and look at the events and people in your life differently. Receiving the message relayed in this book will cause you to be changed and healed. I know dealing with father-wounds will be difficult, because it will require you to face the pain caused by these wounds; however, it is the only way to receive your healing. I just believe that God is putting all fathers and daughters on the road to recovery.

> *When I would comfort myself against sorrow, my heart is faint in me. Behold the voice of the cry of the daughter of my people because of them that dwell in a far country: Is not the LORD in Zion? is not her king in her? Why have they provoked me to anger with their graven images, and with strange vanities? The harvest is past, the summer is ended, and we are not saved. For the hurt of the daughter of my people am I hurt; I am black; astonishment hath taken hold on me. Is there no balm in Gilead; is there no physician there? why then is not the health of the daughter of my people recovered?*
>
> *Jeremiah 8:18- 22*

Wounds of the Fatherless Daughter

Once again, a **father-wound** is *a wound inflicted when a child does not sense the affirmation he or she needs from a father*. By now, the definition of father-wound should be engraved in your soul. As we continue our study of this wound, we want to address those that are suffering silently; namely, the daughters.

In reviewing Jeremiah 8:18-22, we find that the children of Israel are in captivity and bondage. Jeremiah, who was also known as *the weeping prophet*, begins to weep and cry over them. He weeps because he sees God's people being held captive and not making any progress towards freedom. He observes that the men of Israel, who should be taking up the cause for their families, have all turned away from God. The men are out of their assigned and appointed place, and it has an effect on everyone involved.

Because of the actions of the men, there is a profound pain being felt in the hearts of the daughters. In verse 21, Jeremiah comments on the fact that the daughters are hurting, and he identifies with the hurt they are feeling. He states that he is "*black*," which means he is in "*mourning*" with and for them.

He is astonished and amazed that the daughters are aware of what is going on around them in the nation of Israel. The daughters of the nation suffer because their men carry severe father-wounds. The women and daughters of the nation bear the emotional pain of their fathers, husbands, brothers, and sons and they ask if there is no balm in Gilead for them.

A **balm** in biblical times was *a type of salve or ointment used to treat various ailments*. Balm signifies healing; *something that contains healing properties for what may cause you trouble or pain*. In ancient times, balm was used for a number of conditions. Its natural aromatic substances were utilized for healing and soothing. Balm originated from certain resinous plants. During bible history, the area of Gilead was rich in spices and aromatic gums that provided balms, which were exported to Egypt and Tyre and the land of Israel. Gilead was a well-known exporter of balm from the earliest of times.

Balm can also describe or be associated with that of a savior or deliverer, someone or something that can come and deliver you out of your troubles.

Essentially, what Jeremiah and the daughters of Israel were asking for was a healing ointment or salve that could be applied to the scars of these daughters' lives. They were seeking a healing balm that would take away the hurt, pain, suffering, and brokenness they were experiencing. They had developed emotional issues that had been activated and stimulated by something that was missing in their lives. They cried out, because they realized they did not have to stay in the condition they were in at this time. There was a solution; there was a balm in Gilead for them. There was a physician who was able to diagnose their issues and pain.

Were they going to continue to live their life in this state of pain? Were they going to just shut down and not deal with their pain? Where were their fathers?

Factors of the Fatherless Daughter

There are several factors used to identify the "Fatherless daughter" syndrome. According to H. Norman Wright, Five fatherless factors are:

- The 'Un' Factor Factor
- The Abandonment Factor
- The Sexual Healing Factor
- The 'Over' Factor
- The R. A.D. (Rage, Anger, Depression) Factor.[7]

The "Un" Factor

First, is the "***Un***" **factor**. The "*un*" is used when something "*isn't.*" In this case, it is that the daughter has not received affirmation and suffers from a sense of fatherlessness. She feels *unloved* and *unworthy* of the love she seeks. She goes through life trying to make up for the father's affirmation that she lacks. She attempts to earn this affirmation of love using various means. She tries to perform and be good enough to be accepted. The problem is it never seems to be good enough.

The "Abandonment" Factor

A fatherless daughter often feels a sense of **abandonment**. Her father has deserted her and in some ways, she feels it may have been her fault. Along with the sense of abandonment comes the fear of rejection. She fears that she will be rejected by everyone she comes into relationship with. She may superimpose this sense of rejection on every relationship she has. She may have commitment issues, because she does not trust that there is someone who will always be there for her, or who will stay with her.

A woman dealing with an abandonment issue may marry, but will live as if she was a "married single." She may live with someone as if living parallel lives. This is a safety mechanism she employs because of her abandonment issue. It becomes acceptable to live in a house with someone 'like two ships passing in the night'. As a couple, they both may maintain a high level of activity to keep from dealing with each other.

The "Sexual Healing" Factor

Another symptom of a daughter with a father-wound is the **sexual healing factor**. This can run the whole gamut from sexual promiscuity to total avoidance of sex. It can also include the involvement in lesbian activity. This father-wound may have been caused by either physical or sexual abuse by a father or a father-figure. She may continuously get involved in one relationship after another or she may shut down completely. Either way, this is her way of getting even with the one who may have hurt her. She may have been so hurt by a man that she purposes in her heart and vows to never let another man hurt her again. As opposed to dealing with a man, she now decides to share herself with another hurting woman. As women, they connect at the depth of their pain, not so much for sexual pleasure or sexual desire, as this connection goes much deeper. It is the pain of a father-wound that tells her to never deal with another man again.

The "Over" Factor

The **"Over" Factor** is when a daughter *overcompensates or overachieves*. When a daughter who has a father-wound feels a sense of unworthiness, she may overcompensate and go overboard in dealing with other people in her life. She may overcompensate and overachieve subconsciously as a way to show her father that she does not need him. She attempts to convince herself and her father that she never needed him; that she has and can continue to do well without him. She becomes a perfectionist as well. Often, she over extends herself; taking on more than she has time to handle. This can result in obsessive behavior and compulsiveness. She may deal with what is eating her on the inside by excessively indulging in food.

The "R.A.D." Factor

The last factor or symptom is what is classified as **R.A.D.** This stands for **rage, anger, and depression**. Is there a balm in Gilead; is there a physician there?

One woman described the sense of fatherlessness she felt as a volcano that was continually erupting within her heart.

Women who have not had a father-wound resolved might channel their anger and rage into obsessive behavior. They may exhibit a type of obsessive lifestyle or behavior where there is never enough. All of this stems from the rage that is within.

If this rage is not dealt with, it can and will turn upon itself. It will begin to be internalized by the woman carrying the rage and anger and manifest in the form of depression. Everyone experiences some form of depression at some point in their life; however, some women tend to experience such a deep form of depression that medication becomes required in order for them to deal with it.

Women whose rage and anger has turned into depression may develop apathy. Apathy will cause this woman not to care about anything or anyone. In this state, she may say, "To hell with it!" She feels this way because no one understands her or what she is going through. She feels all the weight of the world has fallen on her.

As her husband, you may ask yourself, "how can we have been married for so long and I not know or recognize her state of mind?" You have not recognized this state in her, because she has continued to go through her normal daily activities. She's still driving the kids to school. She's still cooking and cleaning. She's still going to work, school, and church! All you see is business as usual. When she comes to church, we may think her shout is a shout of praise, but more than likely, it is her display of pain and perhaps a cry for help! You have no idea that she has checked out! She has been checked out of the marriage for years, but just has not packed her bags and physically left. How many women have already left their marriage emotionally and only remain physically? What should these women do? How can they begin to find joy again - joy in their relationships, joy in themselves?

Yes, You Do Have Need of a Father

Primarily, a daughter must recognize her need for a father. Secondly, she must realize that the way she feels about herself is directly connected to how her father related to her. How she feels about herself is very much dependent on how she was treated by her father while growing up.

Without a father's affirmation and unconditional love, girls can grow up with low self-esteem and low self-image. The love of a father or lack thereof gives the daughter her sense of worth. Some people do not believe this to be true. They believe that the father is responsible to raise the son and the mother is responsible to raise the daughter. This could not be further from the truth. It is vital that a daughter has a father and a mother in her life.

The father is to bring affirmation to her. He is to render appropriate verbal and non-verbal affection to her. You are, after all, the first male she will come in contact with. If you are emotionally and physically disconnected and removed from your daughter, it will create issues for her. She may develop the mentality that all men she meets will be like you; disconnected, removed from his feelings, and isolated.

Husband and Wife Relationships

Men, how do you deal with your wife as her husband? How does your wife deal with you as her husband? The way you relate to each other may be the result of some father-wounds you both have brought into the marriage. She comes into the relationship bearing her father-wounds and you carrying your own. Fighting and arguing with each other is not the solution. The power of the Word of God will bring the desired healing to both of you. It will bring wholeness to the relationship. After all, it is all about wholeness.

Daughters need to see healthy relationships between their fathers and mothers. They need to witness the daily interactions between their parents- the communication, the laughter, the conflict resolution, as well as their respect and admiration one for another. It is critical for the daughters to see the examples of an affectionate, loving, and affirming husband. Do our daughters observe us honoring our wives? It is important that they do, because how we honor our wives becomes our daughters' reference point of how they will expect a man to treat them. Even our sons need to observe these encounters. They too will learn that this is how a man should honor and treat his wife. He will learn the appropriate way to treat all the women in his life from the example his father sets. Some women seek out potential fathers and husbands based on their material possessions. They look for what he drives, how much money he makes, and the size of his home. Unfortunately, our young girls are growing up with this same mentality.

However, women need to focus less on what he has and more on what he does. Does he honor his mother? How does he relate to his mother? Does he talk about his mother? Even if his mother is no longer living, what does he say about her? The answers to these questions serve as indicators of the type of man you are dealing with. When a man is not talking about either his mother or his father, something is wrong! This should set off a red flag for you. Women, you need to hear him talking about his mother, his sisters, and even his grandmother. More importantly, follow your gut-instinct concerning him. Before you allow your heart to become a part of the equation, investigate the character of the man you are dealing with. Do not let the power of the dollar impair your sound judgment.

Likewise, men, take notice of how she talks about her family. This should help you determine if you should continue pursuing a relationship with her. Does she talk about her father? Is her whole conversation only about her mother? If so, you may be dealing with a woman with a father-wound. She may be a fatherless daughter. Her father may have been absent from her life as she was growing up. There may be something innately painful about the situation where she chooses not to deal with it. The problem with this is that she may be able to put off dealing with that part of her life for now, but at some point in her life, it will surface and she will have to deal with it. Avoidance of an issue or a topic is not resolution. It may not be on her mind or in her speech, but it remains in her subconscious.

When a decision is made to enter a relationship, you have to be open and honest about all areas of your life. Everything should be brought to the table at the beginning of the relationship; the good, the bad, and the ugly. The relationship will not be healthy unless everything is dealt with up front. What you do not deal with in the beginning will eventually come back and deal with you.

A Personal Testimony

My wife, Keira, was the first person I ever knew that was a foster child. I could not personally imagine being an orphan, since that is something that was outside of my realm of experience. She did not know her biological parents, but was adopted and nurtured by loving and devoted parents, James and Rose Taylor, who raised her to flourish and excel. At times, I would ask her if she wanted to meet her biological mother, but she did not see the need. Keira never resented her unusual up-bringing and embraced her unique set of circumstances.

Just recently my wife's heart changed. The season had come where she felt it was time to deal with the "unknowns" of her past. Not knowing what the outcome would be, she decided to begin her search for her biological mother. Dr. Keira said, "Over the course of my life, I became really good at shutting-down emotional hurts, managing to bury issues deep inside only to find them manifesting in unnaturally rapid weight gain, chronic fatigue, and a pervasive unhappiness that would return every so often like an unwelcome house guest." She continued, "I discovered that the pain of disappointment does not disappear on its own and the truth is, that pain left unaddressed will resurrect in your life at the most inopportune times, demanding your full attention."

In a matter of weeks, Keira found her biological mother, and a wonderful addition to her life, Freida Barnes. She allowed the process to run its course. When she decided to seek out her biological mother, I told her I would support her. I did not know how the story was going to end, but I had her back.

I know that there will come a time in your life where you will begin to search out the wounded places in your life. As you search, God is going to release grace over your exploration and allow the necessary restoration and healing to take place. Keira declares of this ordeal, "As for me, God has truly saved the best for last. There has never been any shame connected to my past, just silence. But now there is joy unspeakable and full of the glory of God."

Unhealthy Father and Daughter Relationships

If there is a balm in Gilead; why are our daughters going through so much pain? Why are their wounds not being healed? Why have they shut down?

Let's deal with this topic by addressing three unhealthy father/ daughter pairings. In "*The Father-Daughter Dance*" by Barbara Goulter and Joan Minninger, the authors address several categories of father/ daughter relationships of which I would like to identify three. These pairings will help you understand why we have so many hurting daughters. The three are:

- Lost Father and Yearning Daughter
- Abusive Father and Victim Daughter
- Ruined Father and Rescuing Daughter [8]

First, **The Lost Father and Yearning Daughter Relationship** refers to a father who has for all purposes abandoned his daughter, either physically or emotionally. The father has left his daughter and is perhaps living his life fine without her, but the daughter still yearns for him. There may be a number of reasons why the father abandoned his daughter, however, she blames herself for the disconnection. She yearns for and struggles to earn a father's acceptance. She will do whatever she can to earn that affirmation and acceptance. She desires and needs the heart of her father. A yearning daughter becomes obsessed with trying to figure out what happened. She only wants to understand why her father left. She constantly tries to understand his reasons. She may begin to see her shortcomings as the reason for his abandonment. She becomes convinced in her mind that she is responsible for him leaving.

Daughter, you cannot blame yourself for the decisions your father has made. He is ultimately responsible for any decisions that he makes. It is not about you at all. It is important that you accept this fact. Then, you must allow God to heal you. When you confess to God that you want His help, He will bring healing to your life. When you make up in your mind that you are ready to let go of the pain, God will be there for you to take it away. This is the first step a 'yearning' daughter has to take in order to begin healing.

The Abusive Father and the Victim Daughter Relationship deals with a father who exploits his daughter through physical, emotional, sexual, or verbal abuse. The daughter becomes his victim. She becomes damaged and emotionally challenged, especially if the abusive father sexually violates the relationship. This type of abuse can be much more damaging and traumatic for the daughter. A relationship of incest or molestation usually becomes permanently severed. Just imagine the trauma of a young girl who has been molested in this way by a once trusted father-figure. Without a doubt, this will follow this child through life and into adulthood. It damages a young girl for life and it affects her psyche.

All forms of abuse can damage the stability of a young girl. They are crippled emotionally and mentally by the father who consistently makes derogatory comments to them. Sometimes, words hurt more than the physical pain inflicted upon them. It shouldn't hurt to be a child. It is very sad and painful when a child is hurt by the very ones responsible for protecting them. No father, uncle, brother, or schoolteacher has the right to violate you in any way, ever!

What may develop later on from this is the "victim" daughter. She may grow up seeking other relationships in which she can play the victim. This becomes the norm for her. There are women who are clearly in abusive relationships; however, because of father-wounds, they have come to believe that how they are being treated is the way they deserve to be treated. It then develops into a cycle of abuse. Your mother was abused, you are now being abused, and it is very likely that you will allow your children to be abused. This cycle will continue throughout generations, until someone decides enough is enough.

Fathers, we are not to minimize our daughters because they want to and need to look to us as role models. They want to be able to say, "That's my Daddy and I am proud of him." They want to be able to call us when they go through challenges, knowing that we will be there for them. She needs to know that daddy has made home a safe and secure environment for her. He is there to protect her and to encourage her through all that she may go through in life. Life itself will present our daughters with enough challenges of its own; do not add to it by taking advantage of her.

Lastly, is **The Ruined Father and Rescuing Daughter Relationship**. This refers to a father who earlier in life made the decision not to be responsible for anyone but himself. He was previously a distant father that was completely out there, but now he turns to his daughter for help. The reason he was not there for anyone is that he was on a quick path to destruction. He was not ready to be anyone's father. He was not ready to be anyone's husband. Life for him was a downhill road. He has messed up so badly and is so remotely removed from his daughter that he thinks his life is ruined. Then, along comes the daughter who takes on the role and mindset that she will save her father. She will step in to help him recover and will win his approval and acceptance. She does whatever she can to win the one thing that she has always desired, his affirmation.

The danger in this is that she begins to sacrifice her own well-being in order to win her father's approval. She puts her own life and the lives of her children on hold in order to focus on rescuing her father. She sees this as an opportunity to gain his approval and affirmation. She believes if she tries hard enough she can go back and rescue this man she calls father. She thinks that this will bring him back into her life and will restore their relationship. This type of relationship is unhealthy for everyone involved. She can spend her whole life trying to build something that will never materialize.

Finding Acceptance and Worth

The identity of a daughter finds itself in the father's acceptance of her. The daughter's identity and her self-worth is measured by whether she feels worthy of her father's love. Great damage occurs when the first man in a girl's life fails to acknowledge her worthiness to be loved, and fails to engage her in a healthy manner. Fatherlessness is reflected in the fact that the father may be in the home physically, but he is emotionally detached. Without the father's affirmation and emotional connection, the daughter grows up fatherless.

There are some well-known examples of daughters who have been affirmed by their fathers. These young women live in a manner that reflects the health of their father/daughter relationship. For example, look at the superstar Beyoncé Knowles and the impact her father, Matthew Knowles, has had on her life. Beyoncé is who she is today, because of the affirmation of her father. He believed in her and nurtured her to be the superstar and kind young woman that she has become today.

The same can be said for Venus and Serena Williams. They have excelled and risen to the top of their profession in the tennis arena. What is obvious is that we can see the prominent role their father has played in the lives of these young women. Their father has a place of influence in their lives. He identified their skills in tennis at an early age. He spent time nurturing his daughters to become the tennis champions that they are today.

We can also look at former Secretary of State Condoleezza Rice and the place of prominence she has risen to because of the stability of a father-figure in her life. She had a father-figure who reinforced in her the idea that she could reach as high as she desired. Ms. Rice has achieved great academic success, and continues to possess great influence in the political and governmental arenas.

No father is perfect, but what made the difference in the lives of these daughters is that there was a father who was there; and that

Chapter Four: Discussion Questions

- What mindsets, behaviors and/or relationships do you need to change in order to allow the Balm of Gilead to heal your wounds (Jeremiah 8:18-22)?

- Which of the five fatherless factors lifted up in this chapter are most relevant in your life right now?

- How have symptoms of the five fatherless factors manifested in your life?

Chapter Five

THE TRUTH ABOUT RELATIONSHIPS

Throughout life people will make you mad, disrespect you and treat you bad. Let God deal with the things they do, cause hate in your heart will consume you too.

~Will Smith

The path to true fatherhood is sometimes a steep one. As men, we may find that we have only begun the real journey into manhood when we become fathers. During our growth into fatherhood, we will often miss the mark and wonder why it seems so hard. We may wonder why we are not competent and so unsure when it comes to this thing called 'fathering'. Why do a lot of us seem to fall short in the fatherhood department? Why did someone not teach us how to father these children? The answer to all of our questions is simple;

there is a father-wound in our lives. Most men, who have suffered father-wounds, suffered them because their own fathers had not been fathered.

As I mentioned earlier, I did not meet my father until I was 13 years old. Although my mother made sure that my brothers and I had strong male role models around, such as my grandfather and uncles, I still always wanted to connect with my biological father. I had questions. I wanted to know him, and I wanted him to know me. Finally meeting my father became a pivotal point in my life. I cannot say that everything was perfect right away as if he had always been there, it did improved. Pieces of the puzzle began to fall into place. As I later found out, my father had only met his dad for the first time when he was eighteen. He and I shared that experience. We are closer now than we've ever been, and I thank God for our relationship. It pains me to think what I would have missed out on if I had given up on my dad out of bitterness. A man's error is not always the result of apathy or a hard heart. Many of us do not know how best to handle fatherhood, simply because we had no model or understanding of how it should be done.

Perhaps the question that needs to be asked is this, how could we expect to adequately father our children when we have not been given the blueprint to do so? Men, yes you have been given the ability to impregnate a woman, but this ability alone does not make you a father.

> *When I was a child, I spake as a child, I understood as a child, I thought as a child: but when I became a man, I put away childish things.*
>
> *I Corinthians 13:11*

A progression takes place as we go from the stage of a child, to a young man, and then to a father. This progression is a rite of passage all men have to go through. It is a process that is also sometimes very painful. It is not an overnight thing, and it is of a certainty you will make mistakes along the way. However, the good news is that you are trying to become the best father you can be. It is in the process of becoming a father that you must not stop at the first stage of a child, because a child does not have the ability to reproduce. As a young man, you may have the ability to reproduce biologically, but you do not possess the maturity. Fathers have the ability to reproduce biologically and they possess the emotional, spiritual, and mental capacity to raise and cover sons and daughters.

Many of us will find we have not been able to progress further in our walk with God and in other relationships, because of the mindset we have concerning our natural fathers. There is a fundamental issue in the case of the abusive father that negatively impacts our relationships with others. We have problems receiving God as our Father, because our natural fathers have marred the image of a true father. In many of our communities if the word father is even mentioned, there is a negative reaction. For many, there is a stigma attached to the word. Something must be done! To provide a solution to this issue, restoration is being released to bring about healing and to give understanding of the importance of the father in the life of his sons and daughters.

Headship

Just in case you did not know, God is a God of relationship. He desires a relationship with you and desires for you to have healthy and successful relationships with others. God reveals Himself through relationships. It is not the will of God for anyone to live in isolation. It is not His will for you to be a 'lone ranger'. Statements like, "I don't need anyone" or "I can do it by myself", are self-gratifying and self-denial statements. Beneath these statements lie a severe measure of pain and hurt. One reason you may feel you do not need or cannot allow anyone to come into your life is because of the pain inflicted on you by a father-wound. You have built up a wall because of a father-wound. Your present relationship may only be a surface relationship because you have not allowed it to have depth. When someone comes into your life prepared to go into the private areas of your heart, your reaction is to shut down and push them away. You will only allow them access and entry into certain areas of your life.

God displays who He is in relationships, and more specifically, in the dynamic of the marital convenant. You only have to read what He pronounces in Genesis Chapter Two, to see the foundation of the creation of relationship. As men, we must gain a clear understanding of this foundation.

> *The LORD God said, It is not good that the man should be alone; I will make him an help meet for him.*
>
> *Genesis 2:18*

> *And Adam said, This is now bone of my bones, and flesh of my*

flesh: she shall be called Woman, because she was taken out of Man.
Genesis 2:23

In Genesis 2:18, God announced that it was not good for man to be alone. He then gave the gift of woman to Adam. Genesis 2:23, shows Adam's reaction to the gift he received from God. This gift, his helpmeet, was pulled *out of* man. He named and called her 'woman' for she was taken out of man. These facts are very critical in the development of men and of fathers. Our core understanding, our mindsets, and our paradigms must be shifted concerning the ordered relationship between the man and the woman.

In a marriage, we have often defined the role of the male as "headship", or being the head of the household. The definition and understanding of headship, for most, has been distorted and twisted. For many men and even some women with a distorted view of headship, it has been used only as a means of control. It has been used to justify the act of domination and subjugation. The view was that I (*man*) am in charge and you (*woman*) are to be submissive to my authority. Many have the erroneous belief that the man was created superior to the woman and the woman was created inferior to the man. Some believe that the woman is to be treated as no more than the servant of the man. For many, headship is synonymous with domination.

Is it Dominion or Domination?

God did not establish relationships with the intent for one

person to dominate over the other. When the husband is referred to as the head, it does not mean he is the dominant one in the relationship. The Bible says that man is called to dominate, to have dominion, but he was not called to dominate alone. In Genesis Chapter One, God speaks to "them" both, the man and the woman, not just the man.

> *Then God blessed them, and God said to them, "Be fruitful and multiply; fill the earth and subdue it; have dominion over the fish of the sea, over the birds of the air, and over every living thing that moves on the earth.*
>
> *Genesis 1:28(NKJV)*

Headship means that the man is the one God holds responsible for the relationship's success or failure. As the head, man becomes the source of the relationship. He becomes the authority or the progenitor of what is released through and in the relationship. Headship in itself is incomplete without the woman. We must understand and receive revelation of what it means when we say the woman was taken out of the side of the man. If a full understanding of this is gained and the full appreciation is grasped, we might be able to walk in the fullness of our headship. The implication of this statement should point to one logical conclusion, and that is in a significant part of our makeup, there must be something in us that is similar to a woman's makeup. There must be a nurturing and compassionate side of us.

A nurturing side of a man? Internalize this statement with an open mind, if you can. I believe God took woman from the side of man for a specific reason and purpose. It was not by coincidence or accident that He chose the 'side' of a man to remove the female part of him. Man in himself would not be able to conceptualize the fact of headship, but he may be able to understand it in the context of a relationship. Men, you cannot be head of anything if you are alone and in it by yourself! The fact that God did pull her out of you, out of your side, could possibly mean she is a very significant part of who you are. Could this actually mean that she is as much a part of you as you are a part of her?

Yes, you are a man. You are still the analytical, right brained and effectual one. All of these descriptions are still a part of your makeup. You are the father. However, as much as you are analytical and authoritarian, there is also a nurturing, compassionate, relational side to you. The nurturer in you gives you the ability to be fluid at times. Being **fluid** means you can be *adaptable and changeable when the situation warrants it.*

Men, we are not just the police and the authoritarian around the home. If you believe that is all you are called to do, you will not be able to properly cover your home. You will not be able to receive, relate, and share the revelation of who your wive really is. If you do not yet understand who she is, the revelation of this has been hidden or veiled from you perhaps because you have allowed a predominant and oppressive mindset to influence you. This mindset has told you a lie concerning who your wife and your children are. When we resist developing the nurturing side of ourselves, we forfeit the beauty of unity, oneness, and harmonic partnership that God intended for marriage.

The Importance of Relationship to God

God has put man and woman in relationship and covenant to allow an exchange to take place. She will make an impartation into your life and you will make an impartation into her life. There is something locked up in the woman that must be deposited into the man. Aha! That is the crucial part of the relationship equation that we are missing. Sometimes the only perception of a man we have is that he is responsible for financially supporting his family. Our understanding of headship and fatherhood must be expanded in order to embrace its true meaning. Single men, you must gain a clear understanding of this now, so when your helpmeet does come along, you will be able to see her as your equal and not your subordinate.

The woman is not less than the man. She is not inferior to and subordinate to him. Even in this day and age, we still hear sentiments echoed that are contrary to this fact. In many churches, the message from the pulpit is, 'Let the woman keep silent; women have no place in the pulpit,' and so forth. These statements are being taught out of context as biblical fact. However, God has said clearly in the scriptures, "I'm going to create *man* in my own image; and I have blessed *them*." Here God is speaking of humanity, which means both male and female. We were created from the dirt and shaped in His image. There is a dimension of God that has been deposited in the male body called "man", but do you really think the male species could possibly display all the glory of who God is? God has also taken a part of His nature and poured it exclusively into a vessel called "woman". There is a part of the dimension of God that is poured into both man and woman. When man and woman come together, they represent the total expression of the Creator in His fullness.

When God created man and woman, He did not create them to be competitive with each other. He created them to be equal, one to another. There was to be only revelation and understanding that we have certain aspects and traits unique to one another. There are certain masculine traits like provider, protector, and warrior that are naturally ascribed to the masculine gender. On the other hand, there are feminine adjectives that can also describe man; words like nurturer, receiver/responder, emotional, relational, and creative. Your wife and children will need you to express the nurturing and relational side of you. When this happens, it may cause you to exhibit a part of yourself you don't normally express. Your first instinct may be to play tough, which is your nature, but if you were honest, you would admit you are just as emotional as the next person. Most men have not come in contact with this nurturing side of themselves, because of a lack of affirmation. They were not told this was permissible. Their fathers did not affirm the fact that it is okay for a man, at times, to be emotional. It was not affirmed that some displays of emotions are okay. Most boys were told that the display of emotion is a sign of weakness.

We are called to bring balance into our lives. We are to balance our spiritual, our personal, and our work lives. There is a purpose for this balance. Balance will cause men to walk in authority and assists them in their ability to nurture those they are in relationship with. Nurturing is no longer just a woman's responsibility, but it is just as important for the man to provide for, connect with, and sustain the relationship with his wife and children.

Husband, It's a Requirement... Love Your Wife

The word of God states, "Husbands love your wives even as Christ loves the church." Men are called to give honor to the woman as a valuable vessel loaded with gifts and extraordinary abilities. In this context, God is attempting to mature and develop men in their relationships with their wives. During various stages of your development, God is going to use your wife to assist in the process, so it is vital that she not be shut down. When I speak of shutting down, I mean do not stifle her natural inclination to talk and share herself, her intuitions, her wisdom, and her purpose. She must be seen and she must be heard. She must be allowed to live out her dreams and walk out her visions. If your wife is shut down, it will cut off a necessary impartation that needs to be made into your life. There are dimensions yet to be revealed and those dimensions are to be released through your wife. The union of you and your wife equips you for many challenges that life will bring. One will chase a thousand and two will chase ten thousand! Together, you can accomplish more.

You should not feel threatened or insecure about your wife's goals. You must understand it is your responsibility as the husband to cover your wife in the pursuit of her visions, dreams, and desires. You cover her by supporting her. If your wife is not following her dreams and the destiny for her life, it is not a reflection on her, but a reflection of your headship.

Your first priority is to your family. Your priority is not how much money you make on Wall Street or Main Street. As a husband, your first ministry is how well you take care of your bride! As you fulfill your responsibility to care for and nurture her, your wife will be activated to pull things out of you. Wives are designed to walk alongside of their husbands to be the mirror we need to show us our blind spots. She is equipped to be the 'seer' of the relationship. It is important that she has a voice in the relationship and that the lines of communication are free and open. Many times, she sees through the smoke screen presented by people and situations that we are confronted with, and provides sound counsel to us concerning the matter. We just need to learn how to first, allow her to speak and then, adhere to her counsel. She has been called and anointed to help you in life.

In the midst of it all, it may seem confusing and you may not understand all the nuances of womanhood. There may be times when you might question why you uttered those two simple words, "I do", but just remember you said it, so do it. Your progression from a child to a young man and eventually into a father will be visible as you matriculate through the stages of your marriage.

Identity Crisis: Who Are You Anyway?

We are called as men to get in touch with ourselves, so we can love our wives wholly. Realize that you cannot love your wife until you first learn to love yourself. Therefore, how can we love ourselves if we don't even know who we are? America is experiencing a serious identity crisis. It is rampant in our communities. There are boys who are trying to be girls and girls trying to be boys. Yes, there is a duality of natures, the masculine and the feminine, but somewhere this was not affirmed, resulting in gender confusion and sexual deviance.

Identity comes from the father. It is the father who brings identity to both sons and daughters. In this hour, God is raising up Spiritual Fathers in this nation to bring things into divine order. Spiritual Fathers are our pastors, bishops, and community leaders who are bringing order to the identity confusion of this generation. You may have been sexually molested, abused, or emotionally challenged by an abusive father, another male or even another female, but you are not condemned by your past. Those past experiences do not have to determine what and who you will become.

The bottom line is that many of us have not been fathered. This has produced a need for men and women to create the impression that they are hard and tough. Many, searching for their identity, will join the military, allowing the military to father them temporarily. The regiment of the military requires a schedule and an itinerary of order in your life. You get up at 5:30 a.m. and do PT (physical training) and various other training during the course of the day. You perform all the things required of you to develop the discipline and the order in your life. There is nothing inherently wrong with the military or contributing to the defense of your country. This is an admirable thing. However, a father's affirmation is still necessary because when it is all said and done, you still will not understand the true nature of relationship without it.

God is dealing with the identity crisis you may be experiencing by putting someone in your life for covenant relationship. A **covenant** is a binding agreement between two parties. A covenant obligates the initiating party to the other. Covenants cannot be broken. They are bound together by love, and love is the most powerful force in the universe. The Bible declares that love never fails. As we grow and develop as men, we must consider all of our covenant relationships. The fact is we need our fathers, our wives, our children, our brothers, our friends. At the end of the day, all we have and all we will take with us are these vital and ordained relationships.

God initiated a covenant with man through His Son Jesus Christ. This was a covenant of love; binding God the Father to our best interests, to our struggles, to every pain, to every fear and failure we would encounter in life. This covenant was signed, sealed, and delivered in blood. This was a sacrificial covenant and the sign of God the Father counting each one of us worthy of His love, eternal blessing, and relationship. Once we accept this loving sacrifice of Christ Jesus, we can embark upon a path of genuine healing and restoration, which in turn, empowers us to freely offer ourselves in service, commitment, and love to the significant individuals in our lives.

Chapter Five: **Discussion Questions**

- How has your view of relationships been positively changed due to reading the information in this chapter?

- What "childish things" (I Corinthians 13:11) do you need to set aside to improve your relationships with others?

- Discuss your understanding of covenant relationships.

Chapter Six

THE FATHER'S BLESSING

My dad had an incredible ability to reach out and teach you to do what you never thought you could do.

~Kim Hunter Reed, Ph.D.

Some events that have taken place in our lives can be traced back to the absence of a father. Even if the father was present, was he emotionally and spiritually connected? I am painfully aware that the subject of the father-wound is an emotionally charged issue. It deserves and demands our attention and much sincere soul searching.

A Tangled Web of Deceit

Again, a father-wound is experienced from a lack of *affirmation from a father*. As explained before, this 'wound' can have a variety of causes that are connected to a father; absenteeism, the unknown father, or even the emotionally disconnected father.

Here, I would like to uncover a less obvious cause for the lack of a father's affirmation. I say uncover, because the reason it may happen is not only alarming, but requires a high level of deception. This deception occurs when a child is deliberately and intentionally misinformed about the identity of their father. This deception can inflict a tremendous amount of damage to the psyche of a child. It can cause severe psychological trauma, which is amplified when a mother, who has the honor and trust of a child, intentionally conceals this vital information. There may be valid reasons why this happens, but usually the reasons are selfish and self-serving. Imagine being wired for years with erroneous information just because your mother wanted "his" name on the birth certificate. The thought of this is staggering. Perhaps it was done because the mother knew "he" had the means to provide a generous amount of support. For some, this act may be incomprehensible, but it does happen very often and can have a lasting affect for years to come.

Mothers, it is vital that you let go of this practice of deception. Children not only have a right to know who their father is, but they need to know. Additionally, fathers have this same right and need. Regardless of the state of the father of your child, it is the honorable and right thing to do. Every child needs to know who 'daddy' is. They need to be in a rightful position to receive the blessing of the father. The fact is that the father has vital gifts to bring and impartation to make beyond the tangible. The father brings with him undeniable gifts - the gift of unconditional love and of laughter, the gift of pride, the gift of self-confidence and self-worth, and ultimately, the gift of hope for a greater destiny and future.

The Father's Blessing

On the other side of the spectrum is that of the Father's blessing. In Genesis Chapter 25, we examined the family dynamics of Isaac, Rebekah, Esau, and Jacob. The main emphasis I would like to point out is contained in one sentence, "Isaac loved Esau, but Rebekah loved Jacob." This statement points toward the establishment of the conflicts that take place later in the life of this family. We quickly become aware of a sense of rejection and rivalry that develops between the two sons. This rivalry and competition reveals itself over the course of time. In the beginning of the lives of Esau and Jacob, we will also see that this was really a preordained situation that would be used to bring about the will of God.

> *And Isaac intreated the LORD for his wife, because she was barren: and the LORD was intreated of him, and Rebekah his wife conceived. And the children struggled together within her; and she said, If it be so, why am I thus? And she went to enquire of the LORD. And the LORD said unto her, Two nations are in thy womb, and two manner of people shall be separated from thy bowels; and the one people shall be stronger than the other people; and the elder shall serve the younger. And when her days to be delivered were fulfilled, behold, there were twins in her womb. And the first came out red, all over like an hairy garment; and they called his name Esau. And after that came his brother out, and his hand took hold on*

> *Esau's heel; and his name was called Jacob: and Isaac was threescore years old when she bare them.*
>
> *Genesis 25:21-26*

We can see that the rivalry between Esau and Jacob did not start from their birth nor was it established as they grew to contend for the birthright, but it began while they were in the womb of their mother, Rebekah. The prophetic words in verse 23, had determined the destiny of the twin sons of Isaac and Rebekah. When the first twin Esau came out of the womb, he was described as *being* hairy and red, but when Jacob, the second son arrived, he was only described as *doing* something. As Esau came out, it states Jacob's hand reached out and caught Esau's heel. The name **Jacob** literally means *heel catcher, trickster* or *deceiver*. Jacob knew something, even as a newborn, about the importance of being the first-born. Their war for a positional blessing began in their mother's womb. I believe the reason Jacob was holding onto Esau's heel was an attempt to be the first one to exit the womb, since the firstborn was always the recipient of the blessing.

To Be Loved

Later, Esau is described as being an outdoorsman; a hunter of game and Jacob is described as a "plain man" who dwelt in tents. According to today's standards, Esau would have been known as a man's man, while Jacob would have been known as a "mama's boy." In spite of the warfare, the subsequent sibling rivalry, or how different their sons turned out to be, there remains the main point of emphasis:

"Isaac loved Esau and Rebekah loved Jacob."

There was an unquestionable difference in how Esau and Jacob were loved by their parents. It was important for both Isaac and Rebekah to love these boys equally. The children should not have been aware of the difference in their parent's affection. Although they may have had different personalities, it was important that the parents' love towards them did not differentiate. I believe Jacob felt a definite lack of love and affirmation from his father. This surely caused a sense of rejection and a subsequent father-wound.

My father-in-law, Rev. Dr. James R. Taylor, had a similar experience, which created a father-wound that he carried for many years. He stated, *"My father believed that your oldest child was different than other children. He felt it so much so that he would treat me different than my brother. I didn't like it. Both my brother and I worked on the farm. However, I was treated as a hired hand, but my brother got a percentage of everything that was sold. I was angry about it until many years later, well into my marriage. Growing up I never spoke with my father about how upset it made me, but he knew. My wife was the one who pulled it out of me. I explained to her how I felt and why I felt that way. That released something, because after that I was able to open up more with my own children. But until that time, I couldn't do it."*

Each child is an individual. Each and every child is fearfully and wonderfully made. It is our job to let them know that they have value. Many men carry deeply ingrained wounds from the emotional neglect or abuse of their fathers. Oftentimes, the emotional pain is never shared. It is buried deep within the inner chambers of the heart and often manifests through self-destructive behaviors and anger. In this time of greater knowledge and awareness, fathers and mothers should be put on notice that the damage done to a child may be irreparable and that they will have to give an account to God of their words and actions.

A Father's Blessing Denied

As the story continues, we find Esau coming in from the field worn out, tired, and hungry. Jacob, as usual, is inside cooking some "stew" or soup. Esau takes one look and decides he wants the stew. Their subsequent conversation becomes the turning point for the rest of their lives.

> *He (Esau) said to Jacob, "Quick, let me have some of that red stew! I'm famished!" Jacob replied, "First, sell me your birthright." Look I am about to die," Esau said. "What good is the birthright to me?" But Jacob said, "Swear to me first," So he (Esau) swore an oath to him selling his birthright to Jacob.*
>
> *Genesis 25: 30-33*

The agreement was made. Jacob gives Esau the stew in exchange for the birthright. Like his mother, Jacob is well aware of the value of the birthright. However, Esau, who took such a casual stance concerning the birthright, missed the implication of its worth. We often hear people say Jacob deceived or tricked Esau out of his birthright, but the scriptures state, "Esau despised his birthright." Esau did not fully understand nor was he fully cognizant of its importance. It did not hold much worth to him. Either he did not realize the full scope of it, or he just did not care. Esau agreed and made the exchange. He traded this "blessing" for some soup!

Years later, in Chapter 27 of Genesis, we find Isaac has grown old. He is losing his eyesight and is almost blind. In the passage of time, Isaac realizes that it is time to release the blessing. He calls his favored son Esau to him in order to release very specific instructions. Rebekah overhears Isaac's request to Esau to hunt some of his favorite wild game, to return and cook it, and afterwards he would give Esau his blessing.

Rebekah goes into action. This is a pivotal time for her and for Jacob. Her quick thinking and action is a decisive moment for her son. I believe she was prepared for this moment. I also believe she goes about this deception to heal Jacob's 'father-wound' caused by Isaac's neglect. In quick succession, we see Rebekah calling Jacob to her and devising the plan to receive the coveted blessing. She intercepts the plan of Isaac, because of her love for her son, Jacob. Again, this is not a coincidence or something that is just going to happen. This was the result of a prophetic announcement that had been given years prior. Divine interception had taken place even before their birth.

Therefore, while Esau is on the hunt, Jacob and Rebekah conspire to deceive Isaac. They go and prepare a meal of savory meat. They dress Jacob in a hairy garment and put the smell and aroma of Esau on him. Jacob then goes in and carries out the deception. Only after a few hesitations from Isaac, who seems unsure if he is doing the right thing, does Jacob finally receive the blessing:

> *And his father Isaac said unto him, Come near now, and kiss me, my son. And he (Jacob) came near, and kissed him: and he smelled the smell of the raiment, and blessed him and said, See, the smell of my son is as the smell of a field which the LORD hath blessed: Therefore God give thee of the dew of heaven, and the fatness of the earth, and plenty of corn and wine: Let people serve thee, and nations bow down to thee: be lord over thy brethren, and let thy mother's sons bow down to thee: cursed be every one that curseth thee, and blessed be he that blesseth thee.*
>
> *Genesis 27:26–29*

The blessing released by Isaac upon Jacob depicts a type of Abrahamic blessing and covenant. This blessing ensures that Jacob will live out the rest of his life with the blessing of his father.

The Five Elements of the Blessing

There are several aspects and elements of the blessing we need to understand. I recently read a book that literally blessed me. In fact, some of what I lift up here was taken from this book. The book is entitled *The Blessing* by Dr. John Trent and Dr. Gary Smalley.

In the book, *The Blessing*, the authors talk about five different elements of the blessing. As we deal with the elements they set forth, we will gain a full understanding of it for the healing of the wounds some have suffered. The emptiness and the void caused by fatherless holes in our hearts will be filled. In addition, we will gain understanding of the affirmation of who we are when we receive the blessing.

According to Drs. Trent and Smalley, there are five elements to the blessing:

- *A Meaningful Touch*
- *A Spoken Message*
- *Attaching High Value*
- *Picturing a Special Future*
- *An Active Commitment*[8]

The Blessing of a Meaningful Touch

The first element of the blessing addressed in the book was referred to as **a meaningful touch**. A meaningful touch not only speaks volumes, but it releases volumes. Meaningful implies that it is of importance and carries weight. The meaningful touch is a substantial part of the blessing. The act of touching is significant to the well being of every human being. The blessing can be released through the laying on of hands or through hugging and embracing. Many writers address this issue by stating that most Americans are 'touch deprived'. We are lacking the innate ability to relate to one another through the act of touching.

A touch shows affection. It shows relationship and a spiritual and physical connection. A research study performed in the early 1980's, determined that in order for most adults to be mentally and spiritually healthy, they needed to be touched between 8-10 times daily. That is why in the midst of church service or corporate settings, at times, we are implored and called to pull away and to embrace one another. There is something about embracing that conveys acceptance and a sense of intimacy.

A father's touch is very important. As a man, you are called to display love to your children through touch. Let me be clear – I am not talking about a touch that crosses any lines. I am referring to acceptable and healthy embraces. It is never permissible for you to violate your sons or daughters physically. If there is a point in your life that your own daughter starts to look good to you physically, you need to get out of that house and seek professional and spiritual help. If any of those kinds of thoughts manifest in your mind, you need to bring them into captivity before you destroy your life and the lives of your family, especially your children. Seek help immediately if you have these unnatural thoughts of affection for your sons or daughters.

Jesus advocated the practice of embracing and touching, especially young children. In Mark Chapter 10 it states:

> *And they brought young children to him, that he should touch them: and his disciples rebuked those that brought them. But when Jesus saw it, he was much displeased, and said unto them, "Suffer the little children to come unto me, and forbid them not; for of such is the kingdom of God."*
>
> *Mark 10:13-14*

The disciples did not understand the significance of the children receiving a touch from Jesus. They began to immediately rebuke those who had brought the children to Jesus to receive His "touch." The reason the children were being brought to Jesus was so He could touch them and make a spiritual exchange and impartation into their lives. Jesus was displaying a spiritual and physical exchange that can only be transferred to someone by the laying on of hands. Whether you understand it or not, the laying on of hands is very important. Through physical touch great spiritual impartation is made and it cannot be understated that the effects of physical touch are not limited to the spiritual realm.

For instance, you may go to a hospital where you come in contact with people with physical and perhaps mental ailments. It has been noted and documented that nothing can bring about the sense of comfort and healing more than a simple embrace, except for medical intervention.

When Jesus took the children in His arms, He put His hands upon them and He blessed them. Jesus touched and affirmed them. He knew the importance of the father's affirmation and blessing. To this day, we practice this affirmation and blessing during the dedication of infants and children.

In Mark Chapter One, we see Jesus dealing with someone with leprosy:

> *A man with leprosy came to him and begged him on his knees, "If you are willing, you can make me clean. Filled with compassion, Jesus reached out his hand and touched the man, "I am willing" he said. "Be clean!" Immediately the leprosy left him and he was cured.*
>
> *Mark 1: 40-42(NIV)*

Jesus is moved with compassion for this man who has leprosy. Not only was He moved, but He physically connected with this man, who according to the traditions of that day should not be touched. However, Jesus touched him. Jesus was not afraid of this man. Jesus did not hesitate to reach out to this man and was not waiting for this man to be healed before making contact with him. Jesus was moved by compassion for this man and demonstrated His compassion by touching him.

In the story of the prodigal son, we see a father who was also moved with compassion for someone in need of affirmation.

> *So he got up and went to his father. "But while he was still a long way off, his father saw him and was filled with compassion for him; he ran to his son, threw his arms around him and kissed him.*
>
> *Luke 15:20 (NIV)*

This is the picture of a son who had wrecked his life and was returning home to make amends. However, when his father saw him from a distance returning home, what did he do? He ran towards him and having compassion for his son, fell on his neck and kissed him. This was a sign of affection, a sign of thankfulness that my son who was lost is now back home. The father needed his relationship to be restored with his son and the son needed his relationship to be restored with his father. Fathers need their children, as children need their fathers. Men, we need our children!

When was the last time you touched and embraced your own child? Your child may not live with you and you may have to travel to the other side of town or cross-country to get to your child, but that should not matter. You need to find a way to touch, hug, and embrace your child. If it takes a plane ticket to get to them or for them to get to you, you need to make the investment in that child. If your child is in the home, you should be hugging and loving on your children on a consistent basis.

When was the last time you touched and embraced your wife? If I could only tell you some of the stories I hear from women in the ministry, you would know why the church is in trouble. If you have a *touch-less* marriage, then you have a *love-less* marriage and something is very wrong. This type of marriage is out of order and is an indication that what you see happening in the natural will eventually, if it has not already, happen in the spirit.

The Blessing of a Spoken Message

The second element they talked about in *The Blessing* was the blessing of **a spoken message** or the spoken blessing. In Genesis, we see Isaac begins to release this blessing over Jacob.

> *So he (Jacob) went to him (Isaac) and kissed him. When Isaac caught the smell of his raiment he blessed him and said, "Ah the smell of my son is like the smell of a field which the Lord has blessed.*
>
> *Genesis 27:27*

Isaac's first comment was about the smell of Jacob's clothing. This was actually a compliment, for it spoke figuratively of a field that was ripe and ready for harvest. Isaac spoke to Jacob as he began to release the blessing over his life.

We were created to be speaking beings. God spoke us into being.

As parents, we must understand that our responsibility is to speak over the lives of our children. We are not called to speak critical words to our children, but we are called to bless them. At times, it seems we are much too quick to criticize and condemn them for their mistakes, but we are called to provide the words of encouragement, hope, and strength that they need. We are called to speak and give direction to and for their lives. In Proverbs, we find just how much power words carry.

> *Death and life are in the power of the tongue: and they that love it shall eat the fruit thereof.*
>
> *Proverbs 18:21*

Abuse is Abuse No Matter What You Call It

How many times have you been in a public place and observed a child misbehave or throw a temper tantrum? Can you recall hearing and seeing the parent's reaction? What you may sometimes see and overhear a parent saying publicly probably pales in comparison to what that child may be receiving privately. Abuse is not just physical, but it can be verbal and emotional as well. These types of abuse can virtually cripple a child for life. Words have a way of building a child up or tearing them down. As parents and adults, we all need to make sure that when we speak to children, we only speak words of encouragement. We have to make sure that we are speaking words that give them direction and build them up, not tear them down. The words that we release should not hurt. We have to speak life, not death into our children.

The Book of James illustrates how the tongue is like a bit within a horse's mouth. James explains how the tongue can be compared to the rudder of a ship. No matter how big the ship, the rudder can turn it in any direction it wants it to go. That is what our small rudder, our tongue, can do to us. We need to use our tongue to navigate our children through life. We need to speak wisdom to navigate them through the storms of the teenage years. We need to speak counsel to navigate them through the pitfall of drugs. We need to speak with experience to navigate them through relationships. We are to speak to them and guide them through the ways of sex, giving them the truth versus what they may hear on the street. You really do not want them to hear the facts about sex and reproduction from anyone else but you. You want to reinforce to your daughter just how precious she is. She needs to hear it from you that she is not to allow anyone to violate her in anyway. You want to imprint in her the knowledge that she cannot allow anyone or anything to throw her off the course and the destiny set for her life.

Nighttime prayers with young children are a time to affectionately touch and hug them as you say prayers with them, affirming their special and unique assignment in life. As you touch them, even in the course of a conversation, this conveys that no matter what you do, nothing will separate you from my love. You must speak over your children continually. If you do not speak, know that even in the midst of your silence, you really are speaking.

The tongue is also compared to a fire. This signifies that if we do not get a hold of our words (our tongue), what we think we are building up may in fact be what we are burning down. So what if they made a zero on their report card, or they made a mistake. Let's not go back to our own school years. Let's go back to our own school years. Let's go back and look at our twenty or thirty year old report cards and the list of wrongs we did at their age. We have been called to extend grace and to be a part of the blessing of the spoken message.

The Blessing of Attaching High Value

The third element of *The Blessing* is the release of self-esteem and self-worth. In Genesis Chapter 27, we hear Isaac releasing self worth to Jacob.

> *May God give you of heaven's dew and in the fairness of the earth (of the earth's riches) – an abundance of grain and new wine.*
>
> *Genesis 27:28*

This element of the blessing provides individuals with a sense of high value and worth. It builds self-esteem. When this blessing is released, it lets individuals know they are valuable in the eyes of others. They realize that there is nothing too good for them. You want your children to know that they are esteemed highly and very valuable to you. The resulting self-esteem established causes them to be able to talk to people and not only show, but also demand respect. They are able to look at others eye-to-eye and not feel intimidated. This blessing provides affirmation that enables one to become aware of his or her own intelligence and capability to achieve anything. This blessing reinforces their creativity and their uniqueness. They are fearfully and wonderfully made! They are so unique that no one else has their DNA or their fingerprint. People may label them, but this does not concern them. They are able to think highly of themselves.

The Blessing of Picturing a Special Future

The fourth element of *The Blessing* is the **picturing of a special future**. This is the announcement of a prophetic future. In Genesis Chapter 27, Isaac released this blessing over Jacob. He has pictured and seen what the future has in store for the son he is blessing:

> *May nations serve you and peoples bow down to you. Be lord over your brothers, and may the sons of your mother bow down to you. May those who curse you be cursed and those who bless you be blessed.*
>
> *Genesis 27:29(NIV)*

Isaac released this prophetic announcement for a very special future for Jacob. This is the kind of prophetic impartation or announcement that will cause one to lift up their eyes in anticipation. The money may not be there yet, the future blessings may not have arrived, and you may still be struggling, but yet, you can lift up your eyes with confidence that the blessing is on the way. This blessing is one you can look forward to and will cause you to excel in ways you could not even imagine.

The Blessing of an Active Commitment

The last and fifth element of *The Blessing* is an **active commitment** to God and to your family. This speaks of committing your ways and that of your children to the Lord. Scripture says to "Train up a child in the way he should go and that as that child grows older they will not depart from those ways." I believe if you love them right where they are and commit your life and their lives to the Lord this blessing will be released. You must be willing to commit your life as the example for your children to follow. There is something about lifting yourself and your children up before the Lord and vowing your life and service unto God. It is important to remember the blessing of the father is the blessing that comes from the Lord.

What Happens if You Have Missed the Blessing?

The blessing is there, but you must be in a position to receive it. When Esau finally returned and discovered he had missed the father's blessing, he was overwrought with grief. He was sorry to have taken his birthright so lightly, but he was still expecting the blessing. It was gone, and there was nothing Isaac could do. The Blessing had been released and could not be taken back. The anguish Isaac and Esau both felt when they discovered Esau would not be the recipient of the blessing is apparent in the scripture.

His father Isaac asked him, "Who are you?" "I am your son," he answered, "your firstborn, Esau". Isaac trembled violently and said, "Who was it, then, that hunted game and brought it to me? I ate it just before you came and I blessed him and indeed he will be blessed!"

> *When Esau heard his father's words, he burst out with a loud and bitter cry and said to his father, "Bless me- me too, my father!"*
>
> *Genesis 27: 32-34(NIV)*

> *Esau said to his father, "Do you have only one blessing, my father? Bless me too, my father!" Then Esau wept aloud.*
>
> *Genesis 27: 38(NIV)*

The coveted blessing was now lost to Esau. In his words, you see that Esau finally realized the significance of losing the blessing.

What Does the Blessing Mean to Us Today?

There are several tools that will help us visualize the blessing and how it relates to us today. We must learn how to apply it in a relationship concept and perspective.

How do we release the blessing over our children in this 21st century? If you are a single mother reading this book, you may ask, "How can I have this blessing released over the life of my son without the presence of his father?"

There is significance to the blessing. The blessing is not contextually a onetime experience. The blessing is the whole backdrop of our lives and how we are even called to rear our children. It seems in this day and age, many parents are totally removed from raising and rearing their own children.

For some parents, children have become a burden or an interruption to a schedule. However, when you understand that children are a blessing from the Lord, you will relate to them in a totally different way.

Male Developmental Stages

Traditionally, studies in developmental stages have focused upon children and adolescents. Somehow, we have failed to explore adult developmental stages, particularly within men. Each stage of development in men is unique with its own peculiar set of mental and emotional needs. While spiritual development is more difficult to track and to foresee in individuals, psychological adult development is predictable and more easily identifiable. What is important to note is that both spiritual and psychological development run parallel, and both need to be addressed and cultivated, rather than addressing one and neglecting to deal with the other. Both spiritual and psychological needs demand our full attention and focus in order to develop and nurture men to health and wholeness.

The 0-12 age group is the age where everything starts; it is the foundation of the life of any person. During this time, we start the discovery of our own self-identity and self worth. Everything we are to become is developed during this time-frame. In this period of growth, we can look at the life of Jesus as an example. We find Jesus developing into the man He would later become. We know about His birth, but interestingly enough there is virtually nothing known about

Jesus, until we see Him again at the age of 12 in the temple. Some may wonder and ask why there is no information in the Bible about Jesus' childhood development. However, at the age of 12, the Bible records the commencement of a new stage of development in Jesus' life. At twelve, we discover that Jesus turns the temple upside down, as He talks to the doctors and teachers of His day with wisdom far beyond His years. When questioned about this, Jesus just says, 'I am going about my Father's business.'

Jesus has been in a process of development under the tutelage of His father; not just His earthly father, but His Heavenly Father as well. Here we see the relationship between Jesus and His Father. Jesus' development during this time in His life reflects the way He has been entrusted, and He is now committed to conducting business on behalf of His Father.

From this point on until Jesus turns 30, there is silence again. The only indication of Jesus' on-going process of development for manhood is found in the Gospel of Luke Chapter 2:

> *And Jesus increased in wisdom and stature, and in favour with God and man.*
>
> *Luke 2:52*

The 13-30 year time-frame represents an important stage of development for men. During this stage of life, we find Jesus growing in wisdom and stature and in favor with God and man. Some of you may think at the age of 18 or 22 you have life completely figured out. However, in the Biblical record it appears that during these years, Jesus is not in conflict with others or with authority; rather, we find him having favor with those in His community. Rebellion, insubordination, and chaos do not reflect Jesus' life during the ages of 13 to 30.

Consider the fact that Jesus did not begin His earthly ministry until the age of thirty. There is a great wisdom to be gleaned here. Ages 13-30 are actually a time of preparation for adulthood. I believe that thirty is actually the age around which adolescence ends and true adulthood begins. Therefore, in reality, parents are guiding and grooming their adult children into "adulthood" well after eighteen or even twenty-one. Furthermore, no matter what age or stage of development, the affirmation of the father is critical to healthy development and self-image. Where there is no affirmation of the father, the 13-30 year old will manifest conflict after conflict with those he is in relationship with and with those in authority. Instability, unchecked anger, and violence characterize young men at this age with open father-wounds.

As this chapter concludes, I would be remiss not to address those who have never had a father in their life. Some of you reading this book may never have known your father nor had a father-figure in your life to look up to or receive from. You may never have been in a real relationship with any father, but I want you to know that supernaturally, you can tap into the blessings of your Heavenly Father. God will be that Father to the one who is fatherless. You may think you have missed out, but I declare unto you that it is not too late to fulfill your purpose in life. It is not too late to have your Kingdom of God assignment activated and released in your life for the glory of God.

Within the 30-40 year time-frame the father-wound buries itself deeply and is intentionally suppressed, since the man is busy going out into the world to be the best provider that he can be. The man in this age group is into heavy role-playing. This is the young man who experiences the tremendous weight and burden of carrying huge financial responsibilities not only for himself, but also for a wife or significant other and children. This is no easy task. Therefore, dealing with the emotional pains of life is not his highest priority. The conflict here manifests when the symptoms of the father-wound surface in destructive behaviors like domestic violence, sexual addictions, and deviance. These behaviors are evidence that there is an open wound demanding attention and healing. Men in this age group should know that juggling responsibilities and relationships is a common struggle during any stage of life, but particularly for this age group. Secondly, men in this age group should know that it is important to reach out to others when situations and relationship struggles become overwhelming. You need to know that giving up is not an option, but also that isolation and silence can and will defeat you. Reach out to mature and experienced men. There is help available.

The 40-50 age group is much more soul searching and introspective. They have to be, since they are in a time of inner turbulence known as mid-life. This is a time when most adults look back over their lives, their accomplishments, and work, and make serious evaluations. Is my life meaningful and satisfying, or do I want to chart a new course? In essence, do I want a new life; another life? Is my marriage satisfying, or do I want to start all over? Mid-life is said to be an extension of the chaotic adolescent years, full of self-deception and minefields. This is the age when most men are ready to deal with the pain of their past, since emotional pain marks this critical passage in life. This would be a great time to begin dealing with open father-wounds, since there is time and energy available to correct wrongs, to forgive, to renew commitments, and to enjoy healthy and harmonious relationships, at least for the second half of your life. By this stage of the game, you know two things: 1. You know that at the end of the day, the highest priority must be given to relationships- this is the greatest blessing of life; not money, career, or material things. 2. You have lived long enough to know that what you do not deal with will eventually deal with you!

During the 50-60 year time-frame men have lived enough to truly possess an authentic wisdom. The wisdom they receive is a result of years of testing, trial, and struggle through relationships. Life has seasoned them to the degree that they are fluid in a way that would have been foreign to them in their thirties. By fluid, I mean these men are now able to become the nurturers they could have never been in their earlier stages of adult development. Not only are they nurturers, they are able to emotionally connect, to verbalize, and reach out to others in new ways. Men in this age group have mellowed from their former insecurities and their need to be the dominant one and the controller in their relationships. They are able now to sit back and allow others to shine and release their gifts. There is an easier flow with their wives at this stage of the game, since they are not easily intimidated by the gifts and contributions they bring to the table. The father-wound is more easily identified and healed in this stage of life, since there is no manhood to prove or insecurity to protect.

The sixty and beyond age group represent the wise stages of our communities. These are men who possess the greatest ability to heal others suffering in silence from the father-wound. Men at this stage in life become the Spiritual Fathers and mentors who provide leadership and guidance in assisting young men in finding a place of peace and wholeness along their journey to healing.

You were not a mistake! You are not waiting for your life to pass you by to arrive at the grave! God is about to heal the father-wound in your life. God wants to heal all your pain and all your hurt and heartache. Even when your mind wanders back to what was or was not there; God is going to fill it with His presence. You will walk from this day forward completely whole. The damage done over the years with your father can, without a doubt, distort your relationship with your Heavenly Father, but God has given us grace. The grace provides understanding that even if our earthly fathers were not perfect, healing can take place when the issue of the father-wound is articulated, understood, and addressed.

No Longer Blame, Just Hope

It is important to note one more thing. Many of us are on a father-quest, which manifests in seeking out father-figure substitutes. Sometimes, we find father-figure substitutes in gang leaders, in criminals, and in other poor representatives of manhood. Though these father-figures may temporarily fill the need of the father-wound, for good and for bad; ultimately, they are not the answer you need. There is something about having God-ordained relationships with significant men of character and integrity who can speak into your life and destiny.

The father-wound, if left unattended, can lead you to very lonely and difficult places in your life – divorce, incarceration, emotional detachment, and alienation from friends and loved ones. To open the door to healing and restoration there is an exchange that must take place. Exchange blame for forgiveness, anger for peace, and depression and despair for hope, always remembering a better tomorrow can begin today.

Chapter Six: Discussion Questions

- Think about the statement "wounded people, wound people". In what ways can you, once you have gone through your own healing process, make a difference in your family, community, and the next generation of the fatherless?

- After reading this chapter, what statements and/or thoughts do you no longer believe (for example "I'm a mistake")? Write down the statements on a separate sheet of paper and rip it up as a sign that those words, by the power of God, no longer have control over you.

- What can you do to begin the process of exchanging blame for forgiveness, anger for peace, and despair and depression for hope?

Chapter Seven

EMOTIONAL CONNECTION

"Your kids are your identity; kids mirror you. So if your kids don't see you, who are they going to mirror?"

~Kirk Franklin

The father-wound can affect all of us, male and female. For many, these wounds are emotionally inflicted. As we look at our family structure today, we may find a correlation in the methods we are using to raise our children. We find that we are raising them in much the same way we were raised ourselves. In some cases, this may be a good thing, but there is a link to this process that needs to be viewed. Although past statistics show fathers were physically in the home, I do not believe that most men were emotionally available to their families.

It is crucial that we be emotionally involved in our covenant relationships; particularly, with our wives and children. Societal norms have collectively taught young boys and men in many ways to be unfeeling. They have been taught not to be in touch with their emotions. The message has been that the outward display of emotions is a sign of weakness. Not only have they been taught not to display emotions, but young boys and men have been programmed to withstand pain, both physically and emotionally. Any women can attest to this fact. It appears that men may have a high tolerance for physical pain, but society has taught them to fight the need to express the raw emotion of pain, loss, or grief. They have been taught to just bear emotional pain and in many cases where there is physical pain, not to seek medical attention.

The difficulty with this line of thinking is, as a man, if you can be in that much physical pain and ignore your symptoms, how much emotional pain have you ignored? Imagine the ramifications of ignoring an emotional condition.

The human body was designed and created to produce indicators (symptoms) that trigger a message that conveys when our body/organs are not properly functioning. The manifestation of any symptom serves as a warning for you to seek medical attention. It is very likely that the longer you ignore the warning signs, the worse the condition will become. The longer you wait to seek medical attention usually results in requiring more intensive and aggressive treatment. Addressing any issue at the onset of the symptoms, or in its infancy stage could prevent the severity of your symptoms and subsequent treatment.

That is why an annual medical exam is imperative. It is the first basic step to a healthy you. You should not wait until a condition progresses to see a doctor. We must make it a priority to have regular medical exams every year. As we grow older, the need becomes even more vital. The average individual in their 20's and 30's may only need a basic exam. This exam is usually sufficient, unless there is a prior diagnosed condition present. Men and women in their 40's may require additional testing, along with the basic exam. In this age group, women require annual mammograms; for men prostrate testing is in order. These are just some recommended guidelines available and established when it comes to your physical condition, but what about your mental health? What standards are available to measure our mental and emotional conditions?

Again, from one generation to the next, men have historically been told not to display emotions that are not considered masculine. Historically and culturally, barring men from emotionality was promoted to help men survive traumatic events in their lives, such as the violence of warfare, daily hardships, and the physical dangers they would experience. Our ideas about masculinity and manhood have emerged as a way to help the species survive through the ages. A negative outcome and result of this dominant view of masculinity has been the emotional detachment and disconnection of men from significant others. From early childhood, boys and men are being taught and programmed by the very limiting historical and cultural concept of manhood. The result of this appears to be that it has become practically impossible for most men to connect and be available to others emotionally. The point is they have never *checked-in* emotionally, so they have no idea what to do with their emotions. An emotionally detached man cannot support those he is in relationship with because he is so out of touch with himself.

The emotionally disconnected father and husband is easy to identify and describe. As a husband or a father, you may live in the house, but you are really unaware of what is going on around you. You really have no idea of the real needs of your spouse or your children. You think that by providing their essential needs; food, shelter, clothing, and finances, you are doing the best you know how. Even in the midst of attempts by your spouse or your children to seek to draw closer to you in relationship, you may find yourself shutting them out. You do not know how to handle or respond to their need for a closer bond with you. Your response is to reject their attempts. You choose to stay in your shell. As a man, you may be physically there with your family and that's very good, but you have failed to provide for their emotional needs. You are emotionally removed, and this is a major problem for your family's health and well-being.

Emotional Infidelity

Our homes are experiencing emotional infidelity. Emotional infidelity occurs when one spouse is emotionally unfaithful to the other. To be **emotionally unfaithful** means that one spouse will withhold emotional connection and involvement and/or find emotional connection outside of the marriage. Many men do not take the time to value the significance of connecting with their spouse and children on an emotional level. They do not see the importance of it because they think they do not get anything out of it. However, we all have emotional needs, both men and women.

During times spent with my father-in-law, I learned more about his growing up on a farm. His father was present. He provided. He even taught positive values. But he failed to emotionally connect with his family. My father-in-law put it this way:

"My relationship with my father was cold. He just didn't show affection. I appreciate the things that he did teach me. I just wish that he had been more affectionate. That's one of the things I wish he had taught me more of – how to be affectionate. I never saw my daddy kiss my mother, or hug her, or tell her that he loved her."

As fathers, it is not enough just to put food on the table. We need to make sure our families have everything they need financially, physically, spiritually, and emotionally.

As men we are becoming more aware that our families need our on-going emotional involvement and support. We are learning to better relate to and effectively communicate with those closest to us. What do you do when it seems the both of you are on two different pages? What do you do when your children are going through their turbulent teens?

Many men who have not dealt with their emotions will try to govern their house by legalism and rules. This method of control allows them the option of keeping themselves out of the equation. Emotional infidelity is operative when a man does not listen to his wife and when he fails to communicate with her. A husband is emotionally unfaithful when he does not pay any attention to her.

Because of the emotional infidelity, he convinces himself that his wife does not understand him, or what he is going through. He may find himself spending significant amounts of time at work in order not to go home. He will initially focus on tasks and assignments at his job, but may gradually take on more just to keep himself busy. He may even develop an unhealthy relationship with a female co-worker. Before long, he is sharing private things about himself and his spouse that the co-worker should not be privy to. He may continue until he has divulged every private and intimate detail of his personal life. This is a form of adultery that has sprung from emotional infidelity. He may not have committed physical adultery, but he has brought someone into the relationship that is outside of the marital covenant. He has formed an emotional connection and attachment to someone else without being aware of it. At the same time, he is convinced that he does not know how to, or even need to be emotionally involved with his own family.

Men, you must understand you cannot afford **not to be** in an emotional relationship with your wife and your children. If you do not emotionally connect, it will be detrimental for any child being reared in such an emotionless and sterile environment. Remember, you are not running a military camp. You are to be engaged with your family. As their father, you should be the one to nurture, develop, and affirm your children. The effects of an emotionless environment on marriages and relationships can be damaging. But not only that, the effects of infusing your home and relationships with affection and positive emotion can be an immeasurable blessing that you don't want your family to miss out on.

My father-in-law (Pop Taylor) did not bring the same coldness into his marriage and family. He went on to say:

"Though my father never told my mother that he loved her, I do. I tell my wife. Now I tell my wife that everyday – sometimes two or three times a day. She just loves it. And when I stop, she reminds me."

Since Pop Taylor did not get affection from his father, I asked him how he learned to be affectionate with his wife, Rose. He replied, *"I learned that from my wife. The more affectionate I was toward her, the better I felt. I've learned to be like that with my wife. If I'm somewhere with my wife and I see something that I even think she wants, I buy it for her. If I have the money, I do it. If I don't have it, she tells me that it doesn't matter. Our love is not dependent on it. But blessing her is something I want and like to do. I used to tell the other guys on my job, 'I'll be glad when payday comes. I've got a date.'"*

He continued, *"You can't forget birthdays. You can't. To put it all in one statement – you can't stop courting. My grandfather told me that and I didn't understand it at the time. He said 'courting doesn't even start until after you get married'. But he was right. It makes us both feel better. Also, we never go to bed angry. Our home has been full of love and we've been married for 55 years. And like a good wine, it just gets better with time."*

My wife and I consider ourselves blessed to have this awesome couple as a model of a strong loving relationship. When the love you share is clearly shown, it thrives and blesses every area of your relationship and life.

Today's Children

One survey conducted using the responses of parents and teachers showed a disturbing worldwide trend in this present generation of children. The children of this generation are more troubled emotionally than the last. The survey also reported that this generation of children is more lonely, depressed, angry, and unruly. Additionally, this generation of children is more nervous and more prone to worry. They are also more impulsive and aggressive. Another survey reported that this generation of children would be the first generation to make less money than their parents did. Economically speaking, they will not do as well as we did.

Therefore, we are dealing with troubled children who will grow up with less financial stability than the previous generation. An understanding of the need for a healthy emotional atmosphere must be in place in the lives of this generation and their families. If this is not practiced, we as a people may be headed for some serious trouble.

Spirit, Soul, and Body

And the very God of peace sanctify you wholly; and I pray God your whole spirit and soul and body be preserved blameless unto the coming of our Lord Jesus Christ.

1 Thessalonians 5:23

Many people think they do not possess an emotional bone in their body. However, we are all emotional, we just display it differently.

We have to make contact with our emotional makeup and deal with it. If not, we will continue to be emotional wrecks. We must be a people who are ready and willing to allow God to sanctify us and to work on us; spirit, soul, and body.

> *For the word of God is quick, and powerful, and sharper than any two edged sword, piercing even to the dividing asunder of soul and spirit, and of the joints and marrow, and is a discerner of the thoughts and intents of the heart.*
>
> *Hebrews 4:12*

There is delineation or separation between your soul and your spirit. What has happened to some of us as Christians is we have only been taught to take care of the spirit. The **spirit** is the central part of our lives where we commune with God and enter into relationship with God. God speaks and communicates with us in our spirits. However, the **soul** consists of our mind, will, and emotion. As God speaks to us in our spirit, heavenly and earthly communication filters through the soulical part of man. The soul is the part of man where our destiny and purpose is negotiated. The soul is the part of us that either rejects God's higher purposes or embraces them.

Hebrews 4:12 tells us that the Word of God is so alive and so precise that it has the power to cut and separate the spirit from the soul. Many things that we may attribute to the spirit are in reality only acts of the soul. The spirit and the soul can be so closely intertwined that we cannot differentiate between the two. We can be in an inspiring worship service and our spirits become ignited to the point where we come under the misconception that our lives are in balance. In truth, we will find that our lives are out of balance. When this happens, we must allow God to work this out in us. We have to allow Him to deal with each of us individually. We have to allow God to deal with us not just in our spirit, but in our soul and body as well.

It is common knowledge that our bodies have five senses. The five senses are the sense of smelling, of sight, of touch, of hearing, and of tasting. We relate to the world with these five senses. For example, someone in the hospital who has been diagnosed as being in a comatose state may not be responsive physically. In this state, although the body is unresponsive, it still contains life and breath. Whenever someone is diagnosed as comatose, it is imperative that any visitors they have refrain from talking negatively about their condition. They must only speak positively about the outcome of that person's condition. They must only speak of life, health, and strength. Why? Because you are speaking to the spirit of that person. That person may be in a comatose state, but remember their spirit is still alive! The spirit never sleeps. Speak the Word. Speak encouragement. Speak strength.

In the natural someone that is unresponsive is said to be in a coma. However, what do we call it when someone is unresponsive in the soulical realm? Some wives may say you call that a husband! They may say this because many of us as husbands are non-responsive emotionally. In all of us, we are spirit, but we have a soul that must be developed. We have to give attention to our soul. Understand that emotional involvement is a part of your spiritual development.

Beloved, I wish above all things that thou mayest prosper and be in health, even as thy soul prospereth.

3 John 2

Maturity and development in the realm of the soul allows you to embrace your feelings. It allows you to make contact with your way of thinking and your own will. This contact will allow us to succeed and prosper in life. This is the reason God desires for you to prosper and be healthy in your body and your soul.

The danger with most men is that we have been taught, however subconsciously, that we are not emotional beings. However, we are no different from anyone else. All of us have emotions that we display in one way or another. We all have emotional needs, as well as physical needs. As men, if we fail to get our emotional condition in order, we will continue to raise sons and daughters who are emotionally fragile. The putty-like substance in their subconscious does not become as solidified as it should. Emotionally fragile people are left open and receptive to manipulation and control. Men, if we do not deal with our lack of emotion it will eventually adversely affect the state of our marriage. It will affect the emotional well being of our children. It is reflected in the way we raise our children. If we are not emotionally stable, our children may also grow up to be as emotionally unstable as we are. We must take rule over this.

He that hath no rule over his own spirit is like a city that is broken down, and without walls.

Proverbs 25:28

Emotional Deception

There has to be a balance between the lack of emotion and being overly emotional. We all have experienced the whole gamut of emotions such as anger, fear, joy, excitement, and resentment. We have to learn how to rule our emotions, instead of allowing our emotions to rule us. They just cannot govern us. Take control and refrain from acting and reacting to situations based upon how you feel. Take control of yourself and respond to the situation in a manner pleasing to God.

Emotional imbalance is something that is innate within our culture. This is the true picture of the condition of American males, and possibly men all over the world. One day I was perusing through *Men's Health*, a magazine that is considered the best selling men's magazine in the United States. As I looked over the cover, one blaring thing really stood out to me. The cover titles were only focusing on fitness, nutrition, and sexuality. This magazine has a readership of over 40 million readers a month, not including the number of readers who frequent their website. I looked on the cover of that month's magazine and these were the topics that I saw listed relating to men's issues: *The Sex of Your Dreams; Seven Day Plan to Get Back in Shape in Record Time; Thirty Red Hot Sex Secrets; Ten Perfect Muscle Foods; Your Best Body Ever; Your Career Play Book;* and *Building New Muscles in New Time.* Wow, and this is on the cover of the number one selling magazine for men! This magazine addressed numerous issues, but not one single article addressed the emotional aspect of a man's life. I believe this is an area where most men are hurting, and in need of the most help. We are walking time bombs waiting to erupt, because we were not taught how to deal with our emotions. We can safely say, the only emotion most men deal with is anger and that emotion is normally dealt with in an unhealthy manner. The overuse of the one dominant emotion, anger, potentially brings irreparable damage to every vital relationship in a man's life.

Then, I decided to look at what was being offered in women's magazines. I immediately noticed a difference. Topics on the cover of the *O Magazine* consisted of: *You Are Stronger Than You Know – How to Tap Into Your Power and Really Make It* and *Eat Better Live Happier Inside-Out.* The best selling men's magazines are focusing on the outer shell or external issues, while the magazines for women are targeting internal issues first, and then the external issues. This disturbing trend shows us that there is a social acceptance, and perhaps stereotype, that most men are emotionally out of touch. Additionally, the contrast in the focus of the two magazines highlights the fact that there is much work needed concerning the emotional involvement of men in the lives of their families. We have much to do in correcting this issue.

Chapter Seven: *Discussion Questions*

- What does self-confidence mean to you? Do you exemplify the traits of self-confidence?

- What emotions (sadness, joy, fear, anger, trust, disgust, frustration) are difficult for you to express appropriately?

- In what ways can you bring more balance to your emotions to avoid lacking emotion or being emotionally imbalanced?

Chapter Eight

YOU ARE NOT ALONE

We need others. We need others to love and we need to be loved by them.

~Leo F. Buscaglia

But he himself went a day's journey into the wilderness, and came and sat down under a juniper tree: and he requested for himself that he might die; and said, It is enough; now, O LORD, take away my life; for I am not better than my fathers.

1 Kings 19:4

The scripture from I Kings speaks of a man by the name of Elijah. Elijah was an extraordinary man. He was referred to as:

- *The great prophet of God*
- *The prophet who called fire down from heaven*
- *The one who fought and killed the prophets of Baal*

- *The man who had a double portion anointing to leave his son*
- *The one who carried the spirit of revival wherever he went*
- *The one Ahab called the anointed one who troubles Israel*

Despite all these accomplishments, there was another side of Elijah.

As the story goes, one day Elijah went on a journey into the wilderness. He came to and sat down under a juniper tree and there he requested to die! Yes, the anointed one; the prophet of God wanted to die! What's going on? How can somebody be used of God in such an awesome way and find themselves in the wilderness wanting to die? Did Elijah suffer emotional issues? Absolutely! Elijah had an emotional break down. You would think that because Elijah was a prophet of God, because he performed mighty miracles, or even because his spirit governed him, he would not have emotional problems. The real fact is Elijah had a soul just like you and I.

Like Elijah, we can be anointed and prophetic, but we still have issues. We are dealing with some emotions that can cause us to want to check out of here. Our emotions can cause us to have these kinds of reactions. Some are under the impression that once we are saved, once we find Jesus, we will live 'happily ever after'. I wish that were the case. You will experience some situations in your life that will make you think you are in it by yourself. There may be times in your life when you feel as if God is not with you. Do not allow the enemy to lie to you, this is so far from the truth. God is always with you. He is the God of covenant who is there for better or for worse.

Men, it is important that we learn how to relate with people emotionally. We must develop a greater emotional sensitivity and understanding of the shifting from IQ (intellect) to EQ (emotion). No longer can we operate out of intellect, but we must now operate out of our heart. Before we can deal with others, we must first learn to deal with ourselves; with our emotions of anger, bitterness, frustration, and depression.

Many people, especially Christians, struggle with these emotions. Because they are 'Christian', many believe that they are exempt from these emotional struggles. They are the Christians who are 'Too anointed to be disappointed' and 'Too blessed to be stressed.' Yeah, right!

> *Give ear to my prayer, O God; and hide not thyself from my supplication. Attend unto me, and hear me: I mourn in my complaint, and make a noise; Because of the voice of the enemy, because of the oppression of the wicked: for they cast iniquity upon me, and in wrath they hate me. My heart is sore pained within me: and the terrors of death are fallen upon me. Fearfulness and trembling are come upon me, and horror hath overwhelmed me. And I said, Oh that I had wings like a dove! for then would I fly away, and be at rest. Lo, then would I wander far off, and remain in the wilderness.*
>
> *Psalm 55:1-7*

Like Elijah, David was also an anointed man of God. He was called:

- *The sweet psalmist of Israel*
- *The King*

- The mighty one
- The giant killer
- The one of whom they sang, "Saul has killed his thousands and David his ten thousands."
- The Light of Israel
- The one who would sing or play his instrument and demons would run

According to the scripture, we find this same David 'mourning'. He came in touch with his emotions. As great as David was, he too felt overwhelmed. Just like David, you have to learn to acknowledge and recognize when feelings have taken you into a place of emotional despair. Then, and only then, will you be able to deal with and manage your emotions in a healthy and productive way.

You might be saying to yourself, "Things should not be this way; I should be farther along than I am. I am sick and tired of being sick and tired!" Nevertheless, wherever you are, know that you are still in the center of the will of God. Even though you are in the center of the will of God, you will still experience emotions of sadness, fear, and trembling. At some points in your life, you will still feel overwhelmed. You may feel as if your dilemma has overtaken you. You might have said it like David said it, "If I had wings like a dove, I would fly out of here."

Being emotionally involved in the lives of your family does not make you weak. It is important that you get your emotions under control. Your family needs you. You are a husband and a father who needs to be emotionally connected. Children need to know that their father is available to them to assist them in the things that they go through. They do not need a judge or a dictator; they need affirmation and encouragement to make it through life. Even if you cannot solve their problem, they need to know that you will be there for them, until the problem is resolved. We do not want our wives and our children living in a fragile environment we created. They should not be afraid to make a mistake fearing that it will cause us to go off and lose it or reject them because of our own confusion and frustrations with life.

Men, when our wives talk to us about a situation going on in their lives, they just want us to listen. They are not looking for us to solve the problem. They just want you to feel their struggle and pain. They are seeking your understanding. Regardless of the issue, they just want to know that come what may, you are there for them; you will be standing with them. All you really need to say is, "Honey, I hear you. I understand. I care. I'm standing with you, baby."

God is trying to diffuse some of the issues in your life. Some of the problems you are experiencing are not the real issues. The real issue is how you respond or react to the problem. Are you going to allow the issue to eat at you or to get the best of you?

You are cutting your life short when you keep your emotions bottled up on the inside. Don't you know carrying all that stuff on the inside is affecting your heart? It is causing you to have high blood pressure. My father now warns my brothers and me not to hold onto things. He gives part of his testimony that holding pain and grudges inside results in ulcers. Learning to take each day as a new day and not worry about the past has extended his life. That is why too many men are going to the grave early. We have been allowing our unresolved emotional pain and issues to eat us up on the inside.

You may not be able to locate what is happening in your body. You may have an illness that the doctors cannot find or name. Connecting to your spirit and releasing the spirit of forgiveness brings about healing. If you refuse to let it go, it will eat you like a cancer and you will become a bottle of nerves waiting to erupt.

Most people can comprehend the fact that we are going through these growing pains because most men have never been fathered. They are learning this as they go along. What we are reading in magazines is not teaching us how to handle the real issues in our lives. We have to avail ourselves to study the Word of God. We have to be willing to hear the instructions of those assigned to our lives. More importantly, we have to make a connection with those we are in relationship with.

Ask your wife what she really needs. Ask her how you can better serve her. Do not give the answer if she hasn't asked the question. Decide to become an active father with and in your children's lives. Your wife and your children need you. In your present state, it is amazing anyone would want to deal with you. It is sad to be the husband and the father that no one in the family wants to deal with. What if your wife didn't want to deal with you? What if your kids didn't want to deal with you? Men, it is time to change the atmosphere of our lives and of our homes. Your family needs and deserves better from you.

And about the ninth hour Jesus cried with a loud voice, saying,

> *Eli, Eli, lama sabachthani? that is to say, My God, my God, why hast thou forsaken me?*
>
> *Matthew 27:46*

Everyone deals with emotions, even Jesus Himself. In the ninth hour of His suffering on the cross, Jesus cried out. Jesus in fact cried. This is the same Jesus with extraordinary and divine empowerment and who is revealed as:

- *The Almighty God*
- *The Fortress, The Rock*
- *The Warhorse in the Midst of Battle*
- *The Conquering King*
- *The Captain of the Host*

Yes that Jesus! He cried. Real men do cry! You will realize as a man that you have become in touch with yourself when you no longer have an issue with showing your emotions. A man who cannot cry is a man that must be in a great deal of pain; unexpressed pain. We all need an outlet, a way to express ourselves. When we experience situations in our life that we cannot put into words, sometimes tears are the only answer. I have cried during various difficult situations, and at no time have my tears made me feel less of a man.

At one moment of His life, Jesus felt His Father had forsaken Him. Just like some of you may have felt forsaken by your own natural fathers. The Father of our Lord Jesus is The Father who will never forsake you nor leave you alone. You are not fatherless and you are not alone. There is nothing to hide when we are dealing with a God who knows it all. Our secrets and failures are safe with God.

We can trust that God our Father has our best interests in mind. It is important to know that as a man you can safely release your heart, your emotion, and your thoughts unto God, knowing that He can handle our deepest and most private pain and frustrations. He is an awesome, loving, and forgiving God. God simply needs us to forgive ourselves and trust His Guidance and incomprehensible love in our lives. The real question becomes, "Can you handle that kind of love?"

Chapter Eight: Discussion Questions

- In what way has your relationship with your natural father impacted your relationship with God your Heavenly Father?

- How will releasing the pain of your natural father improve your relationship with your Heavenly Father?

- Can you believe and trust the incomprehensible love and forgiveness of your Heavenly Father?

Chapter Nine

SATISFYING THE FATHER-HUNGER

Growing up, I didn't know about families who were missing a father, because there weren't any in our neighborhood. Today over a third of American children are born into single-parent homes.

~Tim Russert

The Spirit of Elijah Has Been Released

My wife and I have been given an assignment to release the Apostolic and Prophetic dimension to the Body of Christ. We have been anointed for this assignment. Personally, I am thankful I have a greater understanding of this specific assignment than I used to. Not only have I been graced with this Apostolic and Prophetic anointing upon my life; I have been mandated to bring restoration to relationships. The spirit of Elijah has been placed upon me. This anointing can be referred to as the 'Elijah Anointing', which brings with it restoration and healing of relationships.

Furthermore, the anointing of Elijah is the 'spirit of revival'. Wherever Elijah went, the spirit of revival followed. I believe anytime we see the word Elijah in the Bible, it can be interchanged with the 'spirit of revival'. The spirit of Elijah brings about reconciliation and restoration of vital relationships.

When we speak of 'revival', we are not referring to the second week in September or a series of meetings held from Monday until Wednesday. We are referring to the appointed time when Heaven invades Earth. It is the *kairos* moment where we literally experience the glory of God in the earth and in the hearts of His people. This is the time when people are strengthened with His might and they begin to do great exploits. Relationships are restored during revival. The hearts of the people are filled with loving God. They develop a love for Him in ways they never have before. Revival is the time of signs and wonders. It is the time when bondage to addictions is rendered inoperable, and people experience incredible freedom and spiritual renewal in their lives.

In the final two verses of the Old Testament, we see the spirit of Elijah in the operation of restoration. When Elijah comes, he will turn the heart of the fathers to the sons and the heart of the sons to the fathers. If this turning of the hearts does not occur, God promises He will smite the earth with a curse. The resulting curse is the lack of relationship, which is prevalent on the earth and has resulted in generation after generation of emotionally wounded men.

There are many children, and even some adults, who are not able to persevere and get to their next level, because of the lack of restoration of their relationships. There must be a progression in maturity that has to take place in our lives for the healing of these father-wounds. We need to make a commitment to restoration, even when it may seem difficult.

The Lord has blessed me to be instrumental in restoring the relationship between not only my father and me, but between my father and the rest of my immediate family. My father mentioned to me that he gave my brother Harold Jr. a key to his place after they reconciled. My dad, Harold, and my brother Bruce are now very close. We all can now come together and enjoy the family relationships that God intended; full of support, peace and inspiration.

My father spoke of how he and Bruce rebuilt their relationship: *"It was slow at first as we got to know each other and eventually we both understood that everything was ok. But now, we talk on the phone every day. I remember one day when we had been talking for a while. He came and asked me what I thought about something. For him to come and ask what I think means a lot to me. All men feel like they are supposed to be able to conduct their own business, but sometimes you need some input; to hear what other people think. Surround yourself with different ideas and options, and then you can pick out the best. That's all I did, and I was appreciated by doing that."*

As we progress in life, it becomes increasingly important to have the opportunity to share what we've learned with younger generations. They need to hear what we know, and it blesses us to tell them. Our hard, earned wisdom can save them from making a lot of mistakes, and allow them to go even further than we've gone.

My father and brother's relationship is proof that restoration is worth pursuing, even if the change is not immediate. It's been a blessing to both of them, and a blessing to me just knowing that they are both better because of the restored relationship.

> *I write unto you, little children, because your sins are forgiven you for his name's sake. I write unto you, fathers, because ye have known him that is from the beginning. I write unto you, young men, because ye have overcome the wicked one. I write unto you, little children, because ye have known the Father. I have written unto you, fathers, because ye have known him that is from the beginning. I have written unto you, young men, because ye are strong, and the word of God abideth in you, and ye have overcome the wicked one.*
>
> *1 John 2: 12-14*

The Missing Element

Very few people are willing to deal with their father-wound, let alone deal with someone else's. We have very little experience in dealing with father-wounds. We know something may be wrong, but we fail to identify it and we never get to the root of the matter. The father-wound in men had not been addressed, because it had not been identified. The father-wound is not a new thing, it is something that as sons, we have been dealing with for generations. Evidence of this is found in the parable of the prodigal son. (Luke 15:11-32)

Most of us have had very limited experience having someone speak into our lives in a way that helps to push us to our next level. Very few women will tell you they have been in a relationship with a man who was completely whole. Many women suffer privately, because the man they married and the man they love has a deep father-wound that has made their relationship difficult. How many women would be able to say they had been in a relationship with a man who was truly secure in himself, secure in his calling, and secure in his relationship with God? A sadder observation is that even fewer of these men are able to understand that they are called to reach back and get those left behind. Few understand they are called to be like Peter who was told that after he was converted, he was to go back and strengthen his brothers. It is the enemy's goal to wipe out every man, particularly before he is able to come into the awareness of the fullness of his manhood.

> *"And he said, A certain man had two sons: And the younger of them said to his father, Father, give me the portion of goods that falleth to me. And he divided unto them his living. And not many days after the younger son gathered all together, and took his journey into a far country, and there wasted his substance with riotous living. And when he had spent all, there arose a mighty famine in that land; and he began to be in want. And he went and joined himself to a citizen of that country; and he sent him into his fields to feed swine. And he would fain have filled his belly with the husks that the swine did eat: and no man gave unto him. And when he came to himself, he said, How many hired servants*

of my father's have bread enough and to spare, and I perish with hunger! I will arise and go to my father, and will say unto him, Father, I have sinned against Heaven, and before thee. And am no more worthy to be called thy son: make me as one of thy hired servants. And he arose, and came to his father. But when he was yet a great way off, his father saw him, and had compassion, and ran, and fell on his neck, and kissed him. And the son said unto him, Father, I have sinned against Heaven, and in thy sight, and am no more worthy to be called thy son. But the father said to his servants, Bring forth the best robe, and put it on him; and put a ring on his hand, and shoes on his feet: And bring hither the fatted calf, and kill it; and let us eat, and be merry: For this my son was dead, and is alive again; he was lost, and is found. And they began to be merry. Now his elder son was in the field: and as he came and drew nigh to the house, he heard musick and dancing. And he called one of the servants, and asked what these things meant. And he said unto him, Thy brother is come; and thy father hath killed the fatted calf, because he hath received him safe and sound. And he was angry, and would not go in: therefore came his father out, and intreated him. And he answering said to his father, Lo, these many years do I serve thee, neither transgressed I at any time thy commandment: and yet thou never gavest me a kid, that I might make merry with my friends: But as soon as this thy son was come, which hath devoured thy living with harlots, thou hast killed for him the fatted calf. And he said unto him, Son, thou art ever with me, and all that I have is thine. It was meet that we should make merry, and be glad: for this thy brother was dead, and is alive again; and was lost, and is found."

Luke 15: 11-32

Three Distinct Men: Three Distinct Father-Wounds

In the parable of the 'prodigal son', we identify three distinct and unique characters in which the thread of the father-wound and fatherlessness is seen literally running throughout their lives. In several events, we find a detached and a wounded relationship with a father in some form or another. I submit that all three of them can be called a "prodigal." The prodigal was not just the son who ran away, as we have always been taught.

This text speaks of a father and his two sons. There is no mention of a female in this household. I will only surmise what this may mean. Certainly at one time, there had to have been a wife and a mother, but in this parable there is no hint of her existence. The following statements are my suppositions and interpretation concerning the absence of the mother/wife in the text.

I can only speculate, but perhaps the father was an oppressive and controlling man. Perhaps he did not allow his wife to have a voice or a say in this family. Perhaps he did not seek or heed her counsel. She was just a non-entity in the equation of this family. This story seems to be just about a father and his sons. There is no record of her thoughts, opinions, or contribution to any of the family crises that have taken place. The mother may have left some time before this happened. Maybe by this time she had enough! Perhaps she just wanted out of a situation that never seemed to change. These are only guesses on my part; however, we may never know what happened to cause this woman to be unavailable to her husband and sons. We just do not know. But what is evident is there is not one shred of the female influence or a feminine touch in this text!

While it is true that there are some things that only a man can do, I submit that something more is needed. Partnership between parents is essential. If partnership had existed between this mother and father, perhaps this text would not have been penned as part of the sacred writ. If there had been a father and a mother working together in agreement, perhaps some of the hardships in this parable could have been avoided.

Nevertheless, in this parable we find three characters and the history of their lives. First, we see the chronicles of the youngest son, then the father, and lastly, the eldest son, in that order. There are also three different plots or scenes taking place that depict a father-wound.

The Wounds of the Son

In verse 11, it states a certain man had two sons. Out of the three, the father-wound is first identified in the youngest son. The youngest son goes to the father and demands to be given his inheritance. It is his birthright, but he was to receive it after his father had departed; however, he wanted it now. What was the father to do? Does he refuse him, does he debate with him, or does he all together ignore his request? No, it seems right away he gives in and acquiesces to his son's demands.

This son's act of demanding his portion of his inheritance was tantamount to the height of dishonor. The younger son is telling his father to give him what belongs to him, because he feels he has a right to it. In other words, he is saying to his father, "I do not want to be a part of this family and I am through with all of you." By his actions, he is declaring he wants to make it on his own. He takes the blessing of the father lightly just as Esau did. He despises his birthright. What would cause a son to be so defiant and disrespectful? Something had to have happened. Maybe a violation of trust took place that produced a severe father-wound. The severity of this father-wound made the son believe he had the right to approach his father in such a way.

It does not matter what a father did or did not do; dishonoring a father is not a light infraction. In Hebrew times, this was the lowest level a son could reach when he dishonored his father in this manner. This dishonor was a real breach in the spirit. The act of this son signified the disowning and disassociation of the son from the father.

Besides, this father was not an absentee father; he was there! Nevertheless, it is evident this son had an issue with his father. This son had a father-wound. The reaction of the son was a reflection of the level of pain he was experiencing.

What Does Father-Wound Dishonor Look Like Today?

If we were to talk to young African American males today about their father, what would you expect their responses to be? Experience has shown me that most are usually in no hurry to discuss their fathers. If they do talk about them, it is not with high regards by most. Some have no idea who their fathers are, so what would they have to talk about. They are in severe need of restoration.

The problem is we may never know what happened between these young men and their fathers anymore than we know what happened to the prodigal son and his father. What we have are men and young boys who are breached sons. A **breach** is *a violation or abuse of something*. Something is definitely out of alignment in the relationship of today's fathers and sons. The alignment and order has been breached and violated.

We are finding sons who feel the need to leave their homes. They no longer feel the need to be a part of their family. They believe they can make it on their own. They are leaving their homes in an attitude of rebellion. They no longer have the attitude or mindset to please their fathers. They now feel they have to prove something to him. Attempting to rival natural or spiritual parents is not a good thing. Furthermore, the need to *prove* something to others is always a sign that you are on the wrong path.

The father of the prodigal son may have had some issues of his own. Perhaps there were issues with alcohol or with other women. The son may have built up resentment towards his father and perhaps blamed him for any number of things. This father may have fallen short in many areas. He may have been the worst father in the world, but the son did not have the right to dishonor him. Dishonor of a father or mother is never acceptable under any circumstance.

The deeply rooted father-wound of the prodigal son caused him to live a reckless lifestyle. He gave no thought to the adverse affects his lifestyle would have on himself or the irreparable damage to his family. His life was unraveling and spiraling out of control by the minute. The wound in his heart was an offense that he could not appropriately manage. His behavior became more and more depraved and reckless.

Once he had received his inheritance, he gathered his belongings and quickly left the home of his father to go as far away as he could. With a newfound freedom from his parental covering, the prodigal son became totally unrestrained. He began to spend his money and use his possessions thoughtlessly. I believe he did all manner of things and sinned in many ways. The Bible calls it "riotous living," indicative of a soul in turmoil and in deep pain. He spent his money recklessly on alcohol, women, and anything else he could think of. He did his own thing in an extravagant way.

Now compare his life with the lives of those we see around us today. They too are spending their money on things that are not of value; the biggest and nicest cars, the most expensive jewelry; the best of the best. There are even men and women doing this who do not have a job, much less an inheritance. There has not been affirmation from a father to tell them how to survive in life; how to excel and succeed. The absence of the father leaves the son with no financial direction or moral compass. The person with this father-wound usually has no appreciation for relationships. The consequences for the reckless, wounded man can be as disastrous for them, as it was for the prodigal son.

The parable of the prodigal son goes on to state that when the son had spent all he had, the unthinkable happened. There was a famine in the land. A **famine** is *lack of the basic necessities of life for a period of time.* There may not have been a famine of money for some, but for the prodigal, it became a life or death situation.

You Can Run, but You Sure Can't Hide

There are many men just like this prodigal son who are running from a relationship with their father. These grown men can be thirty or fifty years of age, but their pain has them running from the reality of their deeply rooted father-wound. If there were a proper restoration of relationship with their fathers, they would soon realize they no longer had the need to run.

It is a dangerous thing to be connected to someone with a father-wound. Someone with a father-wound lacks the affirmation of who they are. An affirmed man does not have to seek proof of his manhood by being involved in relationship after relationship. He does not base his worth in the amount of money he makes or the possessions he owns. Single women and men who are affirmed know they are fulfilled and whole, whether they ever marry or not.

What if the prodigal son had a wife at the time he left? You could only imagine the drama that his issues and decisions would have produced in this marriage. Think of the confusion and the pain he would have brought into the relationship and into his home. His spouse more than likely would have bore the brunt of his pain and his frustration. Everything; the blame, the pain, and his unresolved issues would have fallen upon her.

As the story continues, we find that this son has left the protection of his father, his money is gone, and now he finds himself in the midst of famine, while in the sovereign hand of God. There will be times in our lives when it will rain, and storms will come. We all may find ourselves in bad situations. This young prodigal son, in the midst of famine, found himself in a pigpen. He found himself in a position where he was tempted to eat what the pigs were eating. Imagine that! This son once had the best of everything in life and now finds himself tempted to settle for the worst life had to offer.

We have all been there. It just never made the front page of the paper. It could have been caused by the loss of a job, a divorce, or a legal issue that drained you of everything you had. Whatever the cause, there was someone there praying for you and you were able to make it through.

Fathers and mothers; just don't give up on your prodigals! The jail cell is better than the graveyard! It is sad but true.

The next move of God is not coming from the seminary. It will come from those we call outcasts; those we call "thugs". What we may think is evil; God is going to use it for His good. There is going to be a revival of the five-fold mantles released through these vessels. God is going to use them in mighty ways to accomplish His will in the earth.

The Father-Hunger

We may never know what it will take for someone in a bad situation to come to him or herself, but at some point, it will happen. How low will it take? What is their limit? This prodigal son finally came to his senses. One day, the realization of what he had lost hit him. He was the son of a rich man, and now even the servants of his father's house were in a better position than he was. He realized what he had lost by dishonoring his father and leaving the protection of the blessing.

This son was hungry. He said, "I perish with hunger." However, there was something in him that was greater than physical hunger. The greater hunger he was experiencing was the hunger based upon the absence of his father. *He had a father-hunger.* He had a hunger that was based on not having men and other father-figures surrounding him. He now hungered for counsel, wisdom, instruction, direction, and the affirmation of a father.

Many are dealing with this father-hunger today. Many men and women both suffer from the lack of a father's presence in their lives. They are perishing in their lives, because of father-hunger. There is a longing, a father-hunger that must be addressed. You need your father before you contemplate marriage. You need a father's counsel when you buy your first house. You need a father's wisdom to make the decision where to go to school for educational advancement. You need your father when you have your first child. The ache of father-hunger must be satisfied. This yearning for a father must be filled in order for you to be the man and woman you are called to be.

The Wounds of the Father

There is a sudden shift in this story. The attention has now shifted to the father.

> *And he arose, and came to his father. But when he was yet a great way off, his father saw him and had compassion, and ran, and fell on his neck, and kissed him. And the son said unto him, Father, I have sinned against heaven, and in thy sight, and am no more worthy to be called thy son.*
>
> *Luke 15: 20-21*

Life has a way of bringing out the humility in all of us. There will be times when we think we have it all together, but life surely has a way of bringing us back to our senses. We will not be able to depend on others or our financial abilities to save us from these experiences; only the grace of God will be able to do this for us. We only have to live a short while and soon, we will realize we really don't know it all.

This son came to himself, as he had been humbled by the experiences of his life. There are times when we are not able to humble ourselves, so the experiences of life will do it for us.

We see the restoration of the relationship between this father and his son. In the text, the father runs to his son and greets him even before the son can come into the village. I believe he did this for a reason. Everyone in the village was aware of what had happened years before. There was a stigma attached to this son; one that could have cost him his life. In biblical times, it was stated that if a son dishonored his father or his mother he was to be stoned. The father runs towards the son to protect him from others.

By this father's actions, the son is spared the humiliation from others and the possibility of being attacked. The father did this so that the shame the son had caused would not be exposed. The father goes to the son, with a sense of urgency, when he was yet a great way off.

Maybe for the first time in his life the father realized the part he played in causing this father-wound in his son. Perhaps for the first time the father was able to take ownership of his faults. Maybe he finally realized that his preoccupation with taking care of his possessions and businesses caused him to lose sight of the importance of fathering.

As fathers, we know the importance of taking care of our family. We know that it is our priority to provide for our own. However, this father was negligent in taking emotional care of his sons. He provided 'stuff'for them, but there had been no emotional investment in their lives. He could now see the consequences of being emotionally and physically detached from his children. He saw the devastation and fallout of not being emotionally connected with his sons. He is now able to display the raw emotion and compassion that he probably had never displayed before. He is now in a place that has prepared him to father his sons. The son, who was out in a pigpen, is now back at home.

The father desires to give gifts to this son. The father comes bearing significant gifts. He gives his son a ring, a robe, and a pair of shoes. The ring is symbolic of authority. The robe is symbolic of the mantle for gifting and achievement. The shoes are symbolic of the restoration and recovery of sonship. The father tells his servant to give his son a pair of the best shoes. Shoes represent sonship. You could identify masters and sons from servants by their shoes. The father wanted everyone to know that this was his son and that his son was still a part of his legacy.

"A good man leaves an inheritance to his children's children."
Proverbs 13:22

Children are being used by God to release men to greater dimensions of growth and maturity. This dimension is called fatherhood. Our children need us and we truly need them. The father was wounded when he and his son were out of relationship. The truth is that both father and son, or daughter, are in desperate need of one another. Whatever the extenuating circumstances, a father should go to great lengths to recover the relationships with his children. No matter the relationship drama between adult parents, remember the children are innocent and they should not have to suffer because of the parents' inability to resolve conflicts.

As fathers, we are called to be the greatest blessing to our families. There should never be a family, when the father dies, that is left without a rich legacy from him. A good and responsible man makes sure that even his grandchildren are financially covered by way of inheritance. There should never be a time when a father dies that the family is left with nothing but a funeral bill and debts. A good man leaves a solid financial inheritance, a legacy of good works, and a rich spiritual impartation.

Revival is on the way! As fathers we are called to stay in the game of this life until the end. We cannot become angry and walk off the court because we don't like the way the game is going. It may be easier to run, but we have been given the grace to stay in the battle and win. The danger is when we abort the process. Do not abort the process. You must stand in the midst of financial hardship. You must stand in the midst of the battle in turbulent times. The blessing of God is there to help you overcome life's adversities.

All of us have made good decisions and bad decisions. Regardless of the situation, God just desires to restore relationships. Fathers are not perfect and families are not perfect. If you have children and have failed to connect with them, the time is now, for God is a God of relationships. You may identify yourself as a man of God, but first you must be connected with and invested in your family and your children. You may have made mistakes. You cannot make up for lost time, but you can be the best father you can be from this day forth. Maturing fathers can only change what happens in the future.

The Hardest Wound of All to Heal

The father-wound expressed by the elder brother was subtler and more deceptive than that of the younger. The younger brother's expression of his father-wound was more outwardly expressed; it was bold in its nature. However, the elder brother's father-wound was repressed and hidden. In actuality, he was inwardly just as rebellious as the younger, even though it was not outwardly expressed. He was just the one who stayed in the house.

It would seem that all the younger brother wanted was the money and his inheritance. The elder brother wanted the money and the inheritance too, we see that he did not want the relationship with his father or his brother either. He was not even concerned about the relationship. This is reflected in his failure to stand up to his brother when he dishonored their father. In this parable, there is no mention of his protesting or defending the honor of his father.

He was the eldest and it was his responsibility to protect the honor of his father, as well as help his younger brother. He did neither. He should have been able to provide direction and guidance for his wayward younger sibling. He was silent; he did not say a thing.

The eldest son's father-wound was suppressed and was so severe that when he finally expressed his anger, it was towards the father, instead of the brother. His wound was so obvious and so severe that no one let him know or informed him of the upcoming party. His apathy towards his father must have been evident, because it appears he was not even informed about the joyous return of his brother. The father and the servants were well aware he would not be able to celebrate or rejoice when this news came. The eldest brother would not have been able to receive or understand the meaning of validating this younger prodigal son.

When the eldest heard the sound of the party and the music, only the servants were able to tell him that the party was in celebration of his youngest brother's return home. This produced great anger in the eldest brother; it produced intense sibling rivalry. Anger is akin to murder and it producted the spirt of murder in the eldest son.

I believe it produced the same kind of anger that caused Cain to slay Abel. The news of the father's celebration over the youngest son revealed the deeply hidden father-wound in the eldest.

Unfortunately, there is a sad conclusion to this parable. The anger that the eldest brother exhibited and expressed was not resolved. After the father explained the meaning of the celebration, the only response the eldest son had was, "What about me?" On the surface, it appears as though the eldest son is disturbed that his father had never affirmed his choice to remain with him, and besides that – that nothing was ever done to celebrate his superior choices. However, the truth is that the eldest brother possessed great spiritual pride and self-righteousness. The text exposes the fact that the eldest brother remained with his father out of obligation and not out of an abiding loyalty to his father. Perhaps this older son was secretly angry that he never had the boldness to outwardly express his inward rage towards his father, as did his younger brother. This would be an explanation for the elder son's explosive anger and bitter and unresolved rivalry with his youngest brother.

This kind of father-wound has been reproduced and is reproducing itself today. This father-wound has produced the same kind of anger in those who have been most affected by it. In our cities and in our nations we see this anger. Young men and boys are so very angry because of the father-wounds they have suffered. They are just angry at the world, and it seems their expressions of anger know no bounds.

For them, there was and is no one there; no father to bring

affirmation. In turn, they express their anger in the only ways they know how. The killing, the fighting, the raw violence, and the angry words they throw around to inflict their pain on others is the direct result of father-wounds.

The Remedy and the Solution

A time of restoration has come to this nation with the purpose of recovering these vital father and son relationships. God is visiting our nation in incredible ways. Spiritual Fathers, mentors, and community leaders are emerging with messages of hope to men who are broken, bitter, and without hope. God has not forgotten this nation or this generation. We are in a great time of spiritual restoration, healing, and renewal for men. We are shifting from a nation and a generation of men who insist on using militaristic force, dominance, control, and violence to solve our problems, to a generation of well-balanced, emotionally helathy men. We are discovering that as men, we can sit across from our enemies and use the gift of reason. We can employ our compassionate and nurturing side to serve those with healthcare needs in our nation. We are also discovering that we can have great relationships with our spouses when we seek to have partnerships with them, rather than to dominate them. For men, this is a time of great transition and change, resulting in personal transformation. Greed and excess are taking a back seat to altruism. Finally, as mature and authentically spiritual men, we can say, "*I am my brother's keeper*". No longer can we cling to the fears and the insecurities of the past. Human consciousness is shifting into a time of greater and more harmonious relationships between father and sons, husbands and wives, as well as between and amongst nations. The restoration and healing of the father-wounds in men are critical to this new age and era. It is a new time and season. I welcome the shift.

Near the end of the interview with my dad I asked him a question. I had already asked him about his memories of Martin Luther King Jr. I'd asked him about Obama. He talked a little about these great men, but he didn't say much. I was trying to find out who his heroes are; which men he looked up to most and why. When he said that he could put me at the top of his list; called *me* his hero, I was blown away. There is no greater honor I can think of, than to have my father tell me that I have changed his life for the better. Through my obedience to the Word of God, and through my willingness to reconnect with my dad and build a real relationship, God changed his life, and changed mine.

I thank God for leading me to reach out to my dad. The Lord restored our relationship, and it has been an incalculable blessing to him, to me, to my children, and to our family line to come.

My dad is now a father to more than me and my brothers. Now, other men and women in his neighborhood come to him with questions seeking advice.

Whenever you're ready to restore a relationship, the first step is prayer. Although I may have gone to see my father those first few times out of just a desire to know him and reconnect, that reconnection was successful because God was in it. I'm now in the position to minister to my father because I asked the Lord to be the Lord of my life, and

I daily seek to follow His direction.

God wants us to have positive relationships. He loves us. If your father or your son is at all willing to be in a positive relationship with you, then God will support it. It may not be easy, but He will show you what to do and what to say.

My father, the man I did not see until I was 13, said this, "*Communication is key. You're busy. I'm busy. I know we can't correspond or communicate everyday. But I know where you're coming from. It's part of knowing you and you knowing me, being able to communicate, reach out and touch somebody, and your relationship keeps getting better. Set a point and go for it.*" He went on to say, "*My son Terry has got a tattoo on his shoulder that says 'the sky is the limit'. I looked at that and asked him what does that mean?' But when you look at it, it means all things are possible. You told me [when I asked you how you've been so successful] that it wasn't you, but it was God.*" Pop added, *"but if God's going to take you to that place, you have to be willing to go. Get on your chariot and go in that direction."*

Look at what God can and will do to restore relationships!

Thanks be unto God, who has sent the spirit of restoration and healing for relationships in this hour. There is a remedy; there is a balm in Gilead for those who need healing.

There is a God who will be the Father you never had. He is the God of your healing and your peace. He affirms you this day. He is here to heal every father-wound. He is here for everyone who calls upon Him. Like the prodigal son's father, He will never ask you what you did or where you were, God is just here for you, no questions asked! You do not have to stay where you are. As of this moment, you are no longer a fatherless son.

Chapter Nine: *Discussion Questions*

- How has your understanding of spiritual restoration and your relationship with God as your Heavenly Father changed through the journey of reading this book?

- What changes would you like to see in your relationship with your natural father after reading this book?

- What is your plan to continue to address the father-wound and spread the word to others about the need to address the father-wound?

Endnotes

1. Rodriguez, Kathy, Healing the Father-Wound, pg. 84-85, Pleasant Word Publishing, Enumclaw, WA; 2008.

2. Dalbey, Gordon, Father Hunger, http://www.narth.com/docs/fatherhunger. html, September 3, 2008.

3. Obama, Barack, We Need Fathers to Step Up, Parade Magazine, June 21, 2009.

4. Reiterman, Ryan, Forbes: Tiger Woods is first athlete to reach $1 billion, http://blogs. golf.com/presstent/2009/10/forbes-tiger-woods-is-first-athlete-to-reach-1-billion. html##ixzz0UXQQogKp posted on October1, 2009.

5. Obama, Barack, Obama's Father's day Speech Urges Black Fathers to be More Engaged in Raising their Children, http://www.huffingtonpost. com/2008/06/15/obamas-fathers-day-speech_n_107220.html, posted on June 15, 2008.

6. Taylor-Banks, Keira, The Matriarchal Dimension, 2nd Edition, pg. 80, Expanding Your Vision Publishers, Virginia Beach, VA, 2008.

7. Wright, Norman H., Healing for the Father-Wound, p70-72, Bethany House Publishing, Ada, MI, 2005.

8. Goulter, Barbara and Minninger, Joan, The Father-Daughter Dance, pg. Putnam Publishing Group, Kirkwood, New York, 1993.

9. Trent, John and Smalley, Gary, The Blessing, pg. 29,41,51,63,71,83,103, 121, Thomas Nelson Publishers 1993, Nashville TN.

About the Author

Bishop Banks is the Senior Pastor and the Chief Executive Officer of the Living Waters Christian Fellowship and General Overseer of the Living Waters International Alliance, Newport News, Virginia. He is married to Dr. Keira Taylor-Banks who also serves as Senior Pastor of LWCF. They are the proud parents of Keira Iman and Jordan Imanuel.

Bishop Banks holds a Masters of Divinity and a Bachelors of Science from Virginia Union University. Bishop Banks is a visionary and global leader whom God has gifted with an Apostolic and Prophetic mandate to strengthen the Body of Christ. Through his weekly television broadcast Expanding Your Vision, Bishop Banks powerfully impacts the lives of viewers nationwide. Bishop Banks and Dr. Keira appear as hosts and frequently appear as guests in various regional and national television broadcasts, including Trinity Broadcasting Network (TBN).

RESPECTING SPIRITUAL PROTOCOL OPENS THE DOOR FOR GOD'S INCREASE

BY

DR. KEIRA TAYLOR-BANKS

Spiritual Protocol is a reference to the respect, honor and deference due at all times to those in authority in the House of God. Many believers attend churches that are out of divine order and alignment. These churches are characterized by dysfunction, contention and continuous in-fighting. Dr. Keira Banks presents Spiritual Protocol as a tool and guide to assist pastors and believers in embracing the Biblical mandate for divine order in the local church. Pastors can use this book as a teaching tool in an effort to transition their entire congregations out of chaos and into the Kingdom of God realm of love, light, prayer and divine order. Individual believers will reference this book to ensure that their motives are pure and their conduct brings honor and glory to God.

www.keirabanks.org

DISCOVER YOUR TRUE PURPOSE AND POTENTIAL

IN

THE *Matriarchal* DIMENSION

BY

DR. KEIRA TAYLOR-BANKS

The Matriarchal Dimension is a description of a sphere of authority and prophetic anointing resting upon Spiritual Mothers and women of high spiritual rank.

"There is an anointing residing in the pages of this book. God surely breathed upon His daughter as she kept her appointment with Him daily to complete this equipping tool, not only for our generation and not only a tool to the nations, but a tool for the entire Bodyy of Christ; male and female."

- Dr. Patricia Bailey-Jones,
Master's Touch international

"The book every woman must read!"

- Wendy Fitts, Corner Insight

www.keirabanks.org

The Lily Housing Corporation is the vision of Dr. Keira Taylor-Banks. It provides temporary housing for qualified women with children. It has also constructed its first Lily Orphanage in Chennai, India. The LHC is a public charity registered with the State Corporation Commission of Virginia. It is supported by generous private donors, small businesses and Corporations.

If you would like to further this great work, contact us at:

www.lilyhousing.org

(757) 820-0717